Empowered Personal Evangelism

Dedicated
to
Jean Seymour

And also to special friends at St Sebastian's in Wokingham

Empowered Personal Evangelism:

Growing the church one by one by one

R. Ian Seymour

New Wine Press

New Wine Press
RoperPenberthy Publishing Limited
23 Oatlands Drive
Weybridge
KT13 9LZ
United Kingdom

ISBN 978 1 905 991 63 1

Cover Design by Zaccmedia
Typeset by Avocet Typeset, Somerton, Somerset
Printed in the United Kingdom by
TJ International Ltd, Padstow, Cornwall

Acknowledgements

First and foremost thank you Lord Jesus. All honour, praise and glory to you, for ever and ever.

I want to also acknowledge here a number of people who have had a significant influence on my Christian life and ministry to date, all of which has contributed in making this book possible: to David Rowe for helping to introduce me to Christ and for first igniting my passion for evangelism all those years ago; to Gerry Muldowney (1927–2012) and Barbara Muldowney for taking me under their wing as a new believer and for their faithful friendship and prayer support; to David Rowley for his insightfulness on complex theological issues and for his continual cheerful witness to Christ; to Ken MacDonald and Stephen Abery for their loyalty, friendship and prayer support; and to Andrew Marsden for challenging me to push the boundaries and encouraging me to be more and more open to the ministry of the Holy Spirit.

And I especially want to thank my wife, Suzanne, and our children, Kimberley, Aaron and Bethany for their love, prayers and support. You guys mean the world to me.

Contents

Introduction   9

Chapter 1:   Evangelism *and the Holy Spirit*   13

Chapter 2:   Pre-Evangelism: *Preparing Ground and Sowing
             Seeds*   29

Chapter 3:   Evangelism: *The Message*   45

Chapter 4:   Evangelism: *The Response*   67

Chapter 5:   Evangelism: *And the Church*   83

Chapter 6:   *The Bible and* Evangelism   103

Chapter 7:   *Prayer and* Evangelism   123

Chapter 8:   Personal Evangelism: *Living Out Your Faith*   141

Chapter 9:   Evangelism: *Sharing Your Story*   159

Chapter 10: *Healing and Evangelism: On the Streets in the
             Community*   173

Appendix 1: *Responses to the Top 10 Questions about
             Christianity*   199

Appendix 2: Recommended Reading   207

Notes: 209

Author's final note and Contact details: 214

Introduction

I find that a great many people in the Church today don't really get involved in evangelism, mainly because they think it's a specialist area and they are no good at it: *'I'm not evangelist,'* they say, or *'I am no good in this particular area; it's not my gift. I feel too uncomfortable.'* Granted some people are 'gifted' evangelists, but there is nothing in Scripture or in church history to suggest that the spread of the Christian message and the growth of the church is down to the ministry a few gifted evangelists. The truth is the vast majority of believers did not come to faith because they met with a particularly 'gifted' evangelist. Indeed, if you are a Christian reading this, then the reason, ultimately, you are doing so is because someone – another Christian (or maybe more than one) – got involved in personal evangelism and told you about Jesus. Someone shared the gospel with you, and God used their personal witness and efforts, to draw you to Himself.

The work of evangelism was never meant to be left to just a select few. Evangelism is a body ministry and it very much should be all hands on deck! But evangelism doesn't have to be scary or difficult; it can be fun and exciting; it can be great adventure and it can be very rewarding. In this book I hope to show you how.

This is a *'doing'* book. It's a book about empowering personal evangelism and about encouraging, teaching and training others to also *do* evangelism. There are lots of excellent evangelistic resources and nurture courses available – *Alpha; Christianity Explored; Emmaus*; to name just a few – but there is very little available in the way of teaching, resourcing and mobilising ordinary Christians to get actively involved in witnessing and growing the kingdom. Until now, that is! This book has been written as a practical tool to help equip ordinary Christians to *do* evangelism.

Years ago the then Archbishop of Canterbury, William Temple, made this comment about the need for church members to be actively involved in sharing their faith and spreading the good news: *'The evangelisation of England is a work that cannot be done by the clergy alone; it can only be done to a very small extent by the clergy at all. There can be no widespread evangelisation of England unless the work is undertaken by the lay people of the Church. The main duty of the clergy must be to train the lay members of their congregations in their work of witness.'* That's what this book is all about: equipping church leaders and church members to get involved with doing evangelism and growing the church one by one by one.

For the most part, the church in the UK (and Western society as a whole) is in decline, and the church has seemingly gone into maintenance and damage limitation mode rather than focusing on mission, outreach and growth. God laid it on my heart to write this book. It is my humble attempt to try and address the situation, at least in part. This, then, is a practical book to help empower and mobilise the local church to be fishers of men, and not just aquarium keepers!

You can probably already tell that I am passionate about evangelism. This book is the culmination of twenty years of preparation and experience in personal evangelism and in winning souls for Christ. I want to state straight off, however, that evangelism is God's work from start to finish. It is the Holy Spirit who convicts and converts people, not us. Our task is simply to be sensitive to what the Holy Spirit is doing, and then to go and join Him in the work of evangelism.

There is, however, a growing problem in many of our churches today: Evangelism, which should be part of the DNA of church, has all but dropped off the agenda (even in many of our theological colleges) and many are leaving it for others to *'do evangelism'* or for God to do it himself, and they are not seeking to join Him in this vital work. It is no wonder, then, that for the most part the church in the UK is in decline. (The 2011 census for England and Wales shows a 13% or a 4.1 million decline in the number of people who declared themselves Christian compared to the 2001 census, and this despite the fact that the population increased significantly in that same time period. This should be an urgent wake up call for the church: Prayer and evangelism need to be put back on the agenda again, big time!) We need to pray for the renewal of our churches. We need to pray for revival and for church growth and we need to urgently put evangelism back on the agenda again. Indeed, it should always be part of our DNA. We must not withhold from the world the best news that has ever come into it.

I believe there is a need for this book. That's why I wrote it. There are plenty of theological and academic books that theorise about evangelism, but this book is different and there is nothing else, as far as I am aware, quite like it. This is a very practical book, full of no-nonsense advice, ideas, exercises, challenges and examples of things we can do, individually or as a group, to help empower and mobilise the local church to get more involved in outreach and evangelism, but first and foremost, and before we attempt to do any of these things, we need to pray. Prayer should be central to everything we do – before, during and after we do it. Again, the key to evangelism is being sensitive to what the Holy Spirit is doing, and then to go and join Him in the work of evangelism. In fact, joining God in the work of evangelism is our ultimate act of worship. (Think about it.)

May God bless you and equip you and your church through these pages in the ultimate act of worship: *personal evangelism.*

Ian Seymour
May 2014

P.S. Grab a pen and as you read through these pages fill it with your notes and scribbles and use a highlighter to make any important sections stand out. Make this book your own personal workbook and it will indeed work for you and your church.

Chapter 1

Evangelism *and the Holy Spirit*

'You will receive power when the Holy Spirit comes on you; and you will be my witnesses in Jerusalem, and all Judea and Samaria, and to the ends of the earth.' (Acts 1:8)

Evangelism is God's work from start to finish. In every outreach event or evangelistic sermon; in every gospel conversation and encounter; in every single conversion experience and every case of personal salvation, the Holy Spirit is *The Evangelist*. It is the Holy Spirit who convicts and converts people, not us. Our task is to be sensitive to what the Holy Spirit is doing, and then to go and join Him in the work of evangelism. In fact, the main purpose for the coming of the Holy Spirit in the first place was to empower us for the work of evangelism and to equip us to witness to Jesus. At the end of Luke's Gospel Jesus said to the disciples, *'You are my witnesses... I am going to send you what my Father has promised* [the Holy Spirit], *but stay in the city until you have been clothed with power from on high'* (Luke 24:48–49). Notice that there is a link here between the disciples being witnesses and their being clothed with the power of the Holy Spirit. And again at the beginning of Acts, Jesus said, *'You will receive power when the Holy Spirit comes on you; and you will be my witnesses in Jerusalem, and all Judea and Samaria, and to the ends of the earth'* (Acts 1:8). Notice again the link between *'you will be my witnesses'* and *'you will receive power when the Holy Spirit comes on you'*. The implication is that bearing witness to Jesus is the main reason for our receiving the Holy Spirit, to empower us. As we are told in 1 Corinthians 4v20: *'The Kingdom of God is not a matter of talk but of power.'* The Holy Spirit is the crucial component in our evangelism. We are not called to bear witness to Jesus alone or in our strength; we are called to bear witness in the power of the Holy Spirit. And that means we need to be open to the ministry of the Holy Spirit; asking Him to give us great boldness in our preaching, and to heal and perform miraculous signs and wonders in the name of Jesus (cf Acts 4:29–30).

> There is a story told about a Sunday school class who had been learning the Apostles Creed and then one morning they came into church to recite it in front of the whole congregation. The teacher motioned to the first child who walked up to the microphone and said in a confident voice: *'I believe in God the Father.'* The second child continued, *'I believe in God the Son.'* Then there was a prolonged and awkward silence until eventually a small voice piped up from the back, *'Please Miss, the boy who believes in the Holy Spirit isn't here today.'* I tell this story because that about sums up the current situation in many of our churches... the person who believes in the ministry of the Holy Spirit isn't here today!

I am a Bible believing 'charismatic'. It has taken me years to fully appreciate that God reveals the truth of the gospel, not just through the Scriptures – and I want to nail my colours to the mast here and declare that I believe in the authority and supremacy of Scripture – but also through the power and ministry of the Holy Spirit and through Christians exercising their God-given spiritual gifts. The gospel is communicated both in word (in preaching and personal evangelism) and in action (through practical Christian love and the ministry of the Holy Spirit). I came to faith and spent my formative years as a Christian in the conservative evangelical wing of the church, and as a result I have a deep love and the highest regard and respect for God's Word and for preaching, and indeed the whole of this book is grounded in the Scriptures. Effective ministry and evangelism, however, is not just about preaching and proclaiming the gospel; it is not solely about Word ministry – effective evangelism involves both ministry of the Word and ministry of the Holy Spirit. (I discuss ministry of the Word in Chapter 6: *The Bible and Evangelism*.)

Unfortunately, there are many in our churches today who emphasise ministry of the Word but who neglect the ministry of the Holy Spirit, and, conversely, there are also many who emphasise the Spirit but who neglect the Word. – In the Old Testament, during the reign of King Josiah in Judah, the high priest, Hilkiah, found the Book of the Law in the temple. It had been lost for many years (cf 2 Kings 22:8). Somehow the people of God had lost the Word of God in the house of God! Now how in the world did that happen? Yet that, unfortunately, is a similar story today and there are many charismatic churches that are strong and vibrant in the ministry of the Spirit but who neglect, or are weak in the ministry of the Word. Fortunately, however, there are a few, and I am glad to say a growing number, who keep and maintain the ministry of the Word and the ministry of the Spirit in balance. In my opinion, this is one of the main reasons why Holy Trinity Brompton (HTB), founders of the Alpha Course, are leaps and bounds ahead of other churches in this country in terms of effective evangelism, church growth and continued church planting; because HTB integrate ministry of the Word and ministry of the Holy Spirit in the way they *'do'* church. (At the time of writing and according to HTB's website: since 1985 they have successfully planted, and had their initial church plants also go on to replant, some twenty three churches.[1])

I sometimes wonder, when it comes to reciting the Creed, if some in our churches would prefer to say: *'I believe in God the Father, God the Son and God the Holy Word'* or *'I believe in God the Father, the Son, and the Holy Sacraments.'* (Naughty, I know, but you get the point?) There is still much apprehension, misunderstanding and, in some cases, even rejection of the ministry of the Holy Spirit in our churches today, but this should not be so. We must not quash the Holy Spirit or deny the miraculous. To be effective in evangelism and making disciples there is an urgent need for a revival in ministry of both Word and Spirit. People need to see and hear the power of God's kingdom come here on earth, now, not just in heaven. It is when people hear the gospel and witness the power of Holy Spirit confirming the gospel that they often turn to the Lord. In Acts chapter 9, Peter heals Aeneas who had been paralyzed and bedridden for eight years. Peter said to him, '*Aeneas, Jesus Christ heals you! Get up, and roll up your sleeping mat!' And he was healed instantly. Then the whole population of Lydda and Sharon saw Aeneas walking around, and they turned to the Lord* (v34–35 NLT). The people saw the proof of the gospel before their very eyes and they turned to the Lord. This is what's known as 'power evangelism': the gospel is heard and demonstrated in power through the ministry of the Holy Spirit.

Without the ministry of the Holy Spirit church can become a cold, dry, ritual formality and, quite frankly, dead boring. It reminds me of the Chronicles of Narnia series and the book, '*The Lion, The Witch and The Wardrobe*' by C.S. Lewis, when it's always winter and never Christmas! It has been rightly said of our churches, that all teaching and the people dry up; all Spirit and they blow up, but a balanced diet or a combination of the two; Word and Spirit together and people grow up, that is, they mature into fully-fledged disciples, who are clothed in power and are better equipped and more effective in ministry and mission. Ministry in the power of the Holy Spirit is a subject far beyond the scope of this book to deal with in any comprehensive way. However, there are books listed in the Appendix that I encourage you to read if this is an area of ministry that you want to explore further. For now, I shall stick to our topic in hand: *Evangelism and the Holy Spirit.*

What is the Holy Spirit's role in evangelism?

This book is titled '*Empowered Personal Evangelism*' but what is the Holy Spirit's role in evangelism? As noted a moment ago, evangelism is God's work from start to finish, and it's the Holy Spirit who empowers us to join with Him in this work. The

Holy Spirit creates signs; He provides us with opportunities and nudges us into action; He gives us insights and He communicates His will and purposes for us; and He gives us the ability to speak and to witness. If we try to do evangelism in our own strength then, at best, our efforts just become an exercise in recruitment. But when empowered by the Holy Spirit our evangelism takes on divine authority and becomes a joyful and exciting adventure as God breaks down barriers and penetrates peoples' hearts. We must be open to the Spirit's prompting and leading us this way; as Philippians 2:13 says: *'It is God who works in you to will and to act according to his good purpose.'* We must be tuned in to listen to the Spirit, we must be willing to step out and be used by God in evangelism and we must also be willing to take risks. It's as if God says to us: *'Your gift to me is availability. My gift to you is ability... You go first!'* We must be open to the prompting of the Holy Spirit and be willing to take risks. Let me illustrate this by sharing a recent example of the Spirit prompting me to act, and of me being available and being given the ability to witness in the power of the Spirit.

Five days ago (prior to me writing this), I was in a local pub one evening after work, having a drink with a couple of men that I have been discipling (one of whom has recently made a commitment to Christ and the other is still on the fence). We were talking openly about Christianity and after a while the landlady came over to clear some glasses from a nearby table and I noticed that she was limping. Suddenly, I felt the Holy Spirit prompt me to offer to pray for her healing. For a split second I had a sudden surge of fear in the pit of my stomach but I recognised immediately where the fear came from because it's satan who ministers fear (I don't like to capitalise his name or show his name any respect). The enemy attacks us by creating doubt and fear. But the fear that we feel is not really our fear; it is the fear the enemy tries to put on us to stop us from taking territory away from him. It is the enemy's fear not ours. The enemy is always trying to hold us back, but the key is to keep stepping out in faith. The landlady, whose name I found out is Dawn, chatted to us briefly in passing and so I asked her why she was limping. She told me she had fallen from a horse a few days earlier and she was suffering from sciatica. I then said to her, *'I'm a Christian. Sometimes I pray for people and they are healed, but sometimes they are not. Would you like me to pray for you?'* She accepted without hesitation and so I asked her to sit in the empty chair beside me, which she then did with some difficulty. Wondering what she had let herself in for Dawn then asked, *'How long is this going to take?'* I told her that if God was going to heal her it would be instant. (I figured that if the Holy Spirit gave me the sudden urge to pray for her then that's what He wanted to do.) She gave me a half-smile and disbelieving look. Then, with my eyes open throughout, I laid my hand on her shoulder and I thanked God for her; I thanked Him for His healing power and I claimed instant healing to her back and the sciatic nerve in Jesus name. The prayer lasted only a few seconds. I then asked Dawn to stand up and she felt no pain at all. I asked her to check – she did, and the pain was gone! I then witnessed to her, suggesting that she thank God, and I told her that Jesus was pursuing her and that He so wanted her to be in relationship with him. Everyone was amazed!

I remember someone once said, *'evangelism means handing out invitations to a free party that's out of this world.'* That's what we do when we offer to pray for people who are not yet believers; we hand out invitations with an R.S.V.P. on them. (For more on this subject see Chapter 10, *Healing and Evangelism: On the Streets and in the Community*, and also the recommended books listed in the Appendix.)

Charles Spurgeon, the great 19th century Baptist preacher, said, *'To be a soul winner is the happiest thing in the world.'* I concur with that sentiment. To be a soul winner we need to let go of any wrong thinking that our evangelism depends on technique or strategy (important as these things are, or can be) and, instead, we need to be open to the Holy Spirit's leading, and allow Him to do what only the He can do, and to do it in His timing not ours. *Not my will but yours be done.* Our prayer shouldn't be, *'Lord, bless my plans and bless my work'* but rather, *'Lord, use me as a blessing in your plans and to do your work.'* This is a lesson, I think, all proud human beings (like us, and me especially) learn the hard way.

I remember the first time I led someone to accept Christ; actually, it was two people at the same time (they were a couple). By the grace of God there have been many others since then, but I shall never forget the first time and how the Holy Spirit directed me to lead others to Jesus. I had been a Christian for about two and a half years at the time and although I had often shared my faith and witnessed to people and invited them to social events and outreach meetings and seeker friendly church services, I hadn't actually led anyone to accept Jesus for themselves. In the beginning I tried to do evangelism my way – of course without any success – but when I was forced to step out of the situation and make space for the Holy Spirit... well you already know the outcome. Let me share with you what happened, but first a little background to set the scene.

In February 1996, a Scottish lawyer on a business trip was shot dead in a hotel in St. Petersburg in Russia. He had been an innocent bystander, relaxing in the hotel restaurant, before he was due to leave for the airport and fly back home. He was shot several times with stray bullets from an automatic weapon fired by Mafia hit men who were targeting a gang leader on the next table! It was dreadfully brutal and an extremely shocking and sad affair for the man's family. Imagine how I felt, then, a week or so later, sitting in that very same hotel restaurant and seeing the freshly disguised marks on the walls where the bullets had been.

At the time I was a business consultant and I had been offered a contract, which involved working for two weeks in Russia. (One week to introduce some training and then a month later, a second week to do follow up). Initially, I was excited about the prospect of adventure and visiting a country that I would otherwise, probably, never visit. However, as I started to negotiate the details of the contract I began to have grave concerns. I remember the heavy feeling in the pit of my stomach at the thought of having to spend two weeks alone in a strange country, thousands of miles from home, where hardly anyone speaks a word of English and where (at the time) poverty, violence and crime seemed to be escalating out of control. When I voiced my concerns to the company, I was promised that I would have a bodyguard with me, or at my disposal, 24 hours a day throughout the whole of my stay! Well, to cut a long story short, I had pretty much decided to decline the offer but try as I might I just couldn't shake the feeling that God wanted me to go; that there was a reason I should go. I prayed about it a lot and I tried to argue with God, but in the end He won, as He always does, and so I accepted the invitation believing that God had some unknown task in store for me.

It was late afternoon when I arrived at St Petersburg airport. The deprivation of the country and people was immediately apparent. It was cold (around minus 10 degrees Celsius). I was met at the airport and taken first to the hotel and then to the offices where I would be working so that I could prepare for the following day. When we reached the offices everyone had gone home and after showing me around, my companion went off to make some phone calls. Left alone to reflect on my first taste of Russia, I became homesick and I started to feel sorry for myself. I had been there only a matter of hours and already I'd had enough. I felt desperately lonely and I prayed asking God to get me out of there. I remember thinking, 'I was wrong. I shouldn't have come here. I can't do this. I'll just give them the money back and get on the next plane out!'

Suddenly I noticed a book that I recognised on a nearby desk. I picked it up and read the owner's name hand-written across the cover, 'David Hazel'. (I had already been told he was an American and a manager within the company.) I flipped it open and a bookmark fell out. I picked it up guiltily and saw the bookmark had hand written notes all over it. I couldn't help myself and I began to read David Hazel's personal goals... two words in capital letters jumped off the paper at me; the words simply said, 'SPIRITUAL GROWTH.' As I read those two words I felt the Holy Spirit touch me, like a mild electric charge, and I knew instantly that this was the real reason I had come to Russia, to speak to this man about Jesus and about *'spiritual growth'*. That was the tonic I needed. I felt uplifted and empowered, and I began to pray silently for an opportunity to witness and share the gospel. Moments later I was interrupted. A stranger walked into the office and I introduced myself, to none other than David Hazel. (He had left something behind and stopped off to collect it.) I didn't need any further confirmation; I now knew what the task was that God had in store for me!

For the next few days I got stuck into the work that I was being paid to do and I was able to spend considerable time with David, and with his fiancée, a young Russian woman, named Tanya Blinova, who also worked for the company and acted as my interpreter for the majority of my stay. I found them both to be very receptive and warm people and we soon became good friends.

On my third evening there they invited me out to dinner and this gave us the first real opportunity to get to know each other. Tanya told me that she had previously worked as a translator for an American Evangelical Organisation, and she had spent two years translating parts of the Bible into Russian. When I asked her if she believed in Jesus, she smiled shyly and said yes, and then for the next three hours or so, which carried us in to the early hours of the next morning, our conversation was all about Jesus. I shared with them my own story and talked about my faith and they both asked lots of questions – it was like they had been saving them up! I could see that the Holy Spirit had been ministering to Tanya for some time but she didn't know how to respond. There had been no one for her to talk to, no church as such, no fellowship, just her fiancé David. She had often tried to talk to him about the subject of faith and although David admitted to being a believer, of sorts, he was very distant and had an air of reluctance about him. As the evening came to a close I told them about the incident three days earlier, when I had first arrived and picked up David's book. I confessed to him that I had inadvertently read his personal goal for *'spiritual growth'* and

I told him I believed that God had brought me to Russia for that very purpose. Tanya was really very excited by this but David less so, in fact, it is fair to say he was stunned!

For the rest of that week, every evening after work we went out for a drink or to eat together and each night the conversation was dominated by one subject; Jesus. I listened to both of their life's story, I tried to answer their questions, I shared the gospel openly, and as the week began to draw to a close and my departure imminent, I began to feel a sense of urgency that David and Tanya should make a personal commitment and accept Christ for themselves. I had known all along that Tanya was ready but David was holding back. When I talked to them about the need of repentance, of seeking forgiveness and accepting Christ, David would hesitate and say that he wasn't ready; he wasn't sure; he needed more time. I distinctly remember him saying he felt as though Tanya and I were trying to sell him something and he wanted to know *'what's in it for me'*. (See Chapter 6: The Bible and Evangelism, for some of the many benefits we have in Christ.)

On my last day, which happened to be a Sunday, I sent a fax through to my wife, Suzanne, (email was still relatively new in 1996 and we weren't online back then). In my fax message I asked her to pray for David and Tanya; that they might turn to Christ that very day, my last day in Russia. Suzanne took the fax to church with her that morning and as a result, several people prayed for David and Tanya. (Prayer is the foundation for all effective evangelism.)

That evening, I again felt the urgency to do something and so during dinner I asked them if they were ready to commit their lives to Jesus and suggested that we might all go back to my room to pray. They agreed. However, on the way David became hesitant again as doubts and inhibitions crowded his mind, and I saw the disappointment on Tanya's face. In the end I reluctantly left them alone and went off to my room feeling dejected and that I had somehow failed.

On my flight home I came to the painful realisation that I had been trying to do things my way. I had been too eager to try and 'close the deal.' Instead of trusting in God and relying on the Holy Spirit, I had tried to hurry things along according to my timetable. I wasn't satisfied with just planting the seed – instead I had tried to plant it, water it, make it grow and harvest it, all in a few days. (Sometimes conversions do happen like that, even instantly, but only when the Holy Spirit is at work and not when we try to manipulate things according to our timetable.) I realised how wrong I had been and I repented. I had tried to push too hard for a decision but God never does that. God doesn't push people He pulls them!

Note: (particularly for those with an unbelieving spouse or unbelieving children): If you continually push the gospel on your loved ones – or anyone else for that matter – they are most likely going to become resentful and be driven further away from God. Nobody likes to be cornered, manoeuvred, nagged at, manipulated or treated like a sales prospect. If God has laid someone on your heart, instead of constantly pushing the gospel on them, you should continuously pray for breakthrough and for God's intervention in his or her life… and then be ready to join in with the Holy Spirit when the opportunity presents itself. In the meantime, make every effort to live beautifully and to overwhelm people with kindness and love. As evangelist and pastor, Robby Dawkins says: *'Displaying the love of Christ is a weapon of mass destruction against the opposition!'*

God's desire is for a believer to overflow with the Holy Spirit that we might… *'be filled with all the fullness of God'* (cf. Ephesians 3:19). A container is only full when it overflows. Fullness can only be measured by overflow. God wants us to be so filled with Himself that we overflow God's love and God's Spirit to others. What's more, when we seek to live a beautiful life, when we demonstrate God's extravagant and unconditional love with our own acts of charity and kindness, well then, sooner or later people are bound to ask: *'Why are you doing this?'* And if someone asks a question like that you can bet they want to know the answer… what prompts you to do this, what motivates you? And then we have the perfect God-given opportunity to tell them.

I am reminded here when Bill Clinton was President of the United States and Mother Teresa was awarded a Congressional Medal for her years of humanitarian work in developing countries. Rather than simply accepting the honour quietly the aged nun took advantage of the opportunity to give a public speech in which she criticised the Clinton administration over its policy on abortion. Shortly afterwards a reporter asked President Clinton what he thought about the criticisms levelled at him by Mother Teresa. After a thoughtful pause Bill Clinton replied, *'How can anyone argue with a life so well-lived?'* – Live a beautiful life and let the gospel speak volumes through you.

Colossians 4:5–6 gives us this instruction: *'Be wise in the way you act towards outsiders: make the most of every opportunity. Let your conversation be always full of grace, seasoned with salt, so that you may know how to answer everyone.'* And 1 Peter 3:15 says: *'Always be prepared to give an answer to everyone who asks you to give the reason for the hope that you have. But do this with gentleness and respect.'* In my early years as a Christian I'm afraid I was tactless and intense, and I tried to bring every conversation round to Jesus. Like the Sunday school teacher who asked the class: *'What's grey, has a bushy tail and eats nuts?'* One little boy said, *'It sounds awfully like a squirrel to me, but I know the answer is Jesus!'* In my eagerness to witness, if someone gave me so much as a hint that they were open to the gospel, instead of answering with gentleness and respect and seeking to win them for Christ, I'd end up using dynamite and try to blow them out of the water! But Jesus never did that. Jesus never tried to force the gospel on people and He never chased after anyone. Jesus doesn't push He pulls!

Michael Simpson, in his book, *Permission Evangelism,* looks at the way Jesus interacted with the rich young ruler (in Mark 10:17–23), and Simpson concludes by saying this: *'Christ was evangelizing, but it sure doesn't look like the way most people do it today. Even though it says Jesus loved him, he stood there and let the man walk away. Why did Christ not follow him when he walked away? Why didn't he try harder when this man seemed so eager? Why didn't Jesus "get him saved" before addressing this difficult area of his life' [his riches]?*[2] Jesus didn't chase after the rich young ruler because he knew the young man wasn't ready to turn his life around and follow Him. Jesus never chased after anyone. Instead, He made himself available to anyone who was genuinely seeking to find God.

Coming back to conclude the story of my two friends in Russia: For the next four weeks I prayed for David and Tanya often, as did members of our church at our weekly prayer meetings. And when I eventually returned to St Petersburg I was met by two people who were both very pleased indeed to see me. In the month long interlude the Holy Spirit had very obviously been at work in their lives, convicting and convincing them, and they were both bubbling over with excitement and wanting to tell me all that had happened. A few nights later, I asked them again, if they were ready to accept God's forgiveness and commit their lives to following Jesus. This time David did not hesitate and back in my room, the air thick with presence of the Holy Spirit, I led them both in a prayer of commitment. Then using a pan of water (very unorthodox, I know, but that's all that was available), I baptised them in the name of the Father, and of the Son and of the Holy Spirit. (Obviously not a full immersion baptism – more of semi-soaking – but in God's eyes I reckon it still counts!) It was a very beautiful and precious moment and, as I said earlier, I will never forget it. Unfortunately, the same cannot be said, about me learning the lesson to wait on God's timing. That took a few more years to finally sink it. Some of us learn the hard way!

Three days later I left Russia for the final time and returned to England, having completed my consultancy contract. However, the story doesn't quite end there... One day, several months later, I suddenly became concerned about David and Tanya, and I wondered how they were getting on with no (English speaking) church to go to and no other Christians to have fellowship with.

Empowered Personal Evangelism

All I could do was pray for them and hand them over to God, but I need not have been concerned. That very same afternoon I received a letter (by fax) from David. His closing remarks said: *'Tanya and I are still strong and growing. We are now also expanding our faith and pray together every day. Wow, it's great! God bless. David.'*

Let me say it again, evangelism is God's work from start to finish. The Holy Spirit equips us and empowers us to join Him in the work of evangelism. The Holy Spirit creates signs that point to Jesus. The Holy Spirit provides us with opportunities and nudges us into action; He gives us insights; and He communicates His will and purposes for us. Bill Johnson describes our ministering in the power of the Holy Spirit to being like a surfer catching a wave: *We position ourselves in ministry, look for what God is doing and then paddle like crazy to catch the wave.*[3] There are, however, two major factors that we need to have if we are to recognise the Holy Spirit's leading us in this way: firstly, we need to be living in an intimate relationship with God. If we want to know the Holy Spirit leading us, if we want to know God's will and hear His voice speaking to us, then we need to invest time and effort into developing an intimate relationship with Him. Ministry without intimacy is a ministry without authority. Secondly, we need to ask God to open our eyes so that we can see where He is at work in the life of others, so that we can go and join Him. If we make ourselves available to God and ask Him to show us where to go, and then we are obedient, God will use us, and He will give us the ability to produce much fruit.

We should pray with the psalmist: *'Show me the way I should go for to you I lift up my soul.'* (Psalm 143:8b)

Group Exercise (the following is an excerpt from the Methodist Church evangelism resource *'Talking of God'* which is available as a free download at www.methodist. org.uk/talkingofgod): Read the parable of the sower in Luke 8:5–15 and consider the four soils. Ask the group these questions: What are the key features of the parable of the sower? How might these features help us when we are

---

26

thinking and talking about our faith to others? (Leader's notes: It is important to stress that the mission of God is about what God is doing, and not about what we are doing.) Things to pull out of the text include the following:

- Seed was sown arbitrarily. There is no telling what will happen as a result of a conversation. What is important from the parable is that the 'seed' is liberally scattered.
- Evangelism can work as an intentional and organized campaign, but most of us, most of the time, are faced with everyday situations, which require us to share faith naturally and spontaneously.
- Seeds need the right soil, so too do conversations. Conversations are also about relationship, integrity and authenticity. The people we are, the character we are nurturing through our discipleship and the friends we make are vital aspects to faith sharing.
- For good seed to flourish, it needs to be in the right conditions, otherwise growth is restricted. It is important to run courses which introduce people to the Christian faith in a relaxed, non-threatening way. Courses like Alpha, Emmaus and Start have the potential to provide this framework. The inclusion of a mealtime and table-based discussions are of immense importance in helping people to relax and share freely with one another.
- The seed does not grow because the farmer forces it to grow. So too, people's faith does not happen because we force it to. We need to be able and willing to trust God for growth – and prepared to be surprised!
- The farmer, once he has sown the seed, does not go back to the field a week later and dig it up to see if the seeds are growing properly. Likewise we need to be prayerful and trusting as we continue to share our faith with people. God can do far more than we imagine.[4]

Chapter 2

Pre-Evangelism:
Preparing Ground and Sowing Seeds

In the beginning God created the heavens and the earth.
– Genesis 1:1

Have you ever been fishing or maybe watched one of those engaging fishing programmes on TV? Successful fishermen seem to know when and where to fish as they continually cast out the bait and wait for a bite. But if the fish are not biting the fishermen keeps changing his bait until they do bite or else he packs up and comes back another day to fish again. When a fish takes the bait the fisherman strikes, hooks the fish and then reels it in slowly. All fish put up a fight when they are caught; they don't accept capture easily and they try to resist and wriggle free at every twist and turn. Eventually, though, the fish comes to realise that it's caught and cannot escape and slowly but surely its resistance grows weaker until its finally reeled in and landed. All fisherman will tell you that the harder and longer the fight the bigger and better the catch! Fishermen will also tell you about the one that got away! Fish sometimes escape; they pull loose, snap the line or spit out the hook before it gets a chance to become firmly embedded. Some fish even wriggle free once they have been landed – they are the ones that were never really caught! The art of successful fishing, then, is to be continually casting out the bait, and when you get a bite, strike to hook the fish, and then reel them in slowly and land them properly. The art is not simply about catching fish, it's also about keeping them!

As we set out on this journey together, this fishing trip – this adventure in evangelism – the first thing we often need to do in personal evangelism is to prepare the way for the gospel, just as John the Baptist prepared the way for coming of Christ. Often, but by no means always, people that we meet who are 'seekers' need to start at the very beginning, and this means we have to prepare the ground so that we can then sow the seeds for the gospel. We do this by provoking their thinking, answering their questions, challenging their preconceptions and arousing their curiosity so that they will want to hear more. In this chapter I am going to demonstrate how we can do this by using material from a recent evangelistic lecture I gave on the topic: *'How can I know God exists?'*

Let me start by stating that many people think science and Christianity are at odds with one another and that they contradict each other but I find the opposite to be true; I find that they complement each other. In the final analysis, science only ever seeks to answer the question, *'How?'* but Christianity never attempts to answer that question: Christianity seeks to answer the question *'Who'* not *'How?'* Similarly, many people ask the question: *'How can I know there is a God?'* and they may even turn to the Bible for answers, but the Bible never tries to prove that God exists, it simply assumes it, and from the very beginning. Indeed, the very first sentence of the Bible opens with the words: *'In the beginning God...'* – assuming the existence of God from the very outset. But I want to put the Bible and historical events to one side, for the moment (I will come back to this later), and say that there is a great deal of other evidence or proof for God's existence... proof, that is, for those who have eyes to see it and can accept it as such. In answer to the question, *'How can I know there is a God',* we need to be able to argue that there is good, reliable and overwhelming evidence to prove that God exists. To help us do that I am going to share some facts with you, under three headings – each pointing to the fact that God not only exists, but also that we can know Him personally. You might like to use some of this material as bait next time you go fishing! The first pointer is the fact of the world and of design.

Evidence No.1: The Argument From Creation.

I read a quote recently, from Josh McDowell and Don Stewart, which said, *'Atheists affirm that there is no God. Yet they cannot hold this position dogmatically. For us to be able to make this type of statement with authority, we would have to know the universe in its entirety and to possess all knowledge. If anyone had these credentials, then, by definition, they would be God.'* Good point! G. K. Chesterton put it a different way, he said: *'If there were no God there would be no atheists.'*

In the 2011 census for England and Wales 59% of the population claimed to believe in God and put down on their census form that they were Christian! (This is a 13% decline over the 2001 census and is massive wake up call for the church, which is discussed in more detail in Chapter 3, Evangelism: *The Message*.) Many other people believe in the Big Bang Theory (theory meaning hypothesis, idea, speculation… not fact!) But if it's true and the universe did start with a 'Big Bang' then what made the 'Big Bang' happen? God? It really is ridiculous to suggest that the entire universe just popped into existence for absolutely no reason at all and purely by chance or accident! (That's what I call blind faith!) Consider the following analogy, which I think makes the point well.

> Three men are walking across a vast open desert when they come across a magnificent city in the middle of nowhere in particular, (the Earth in our universe). And the three men marvel in amazement as they wander around and discover that the city is truly astonishing and wonderfully intricate in its design: everything is so perfectly balanced, right the way down to the tiniest microscopic detail; everything is so beautiful and fits so flawlessly together… And so the three men come to ponder and debate upon how this magnificent and amazing city came to be. The first man concluded that he didn't really care! It just *is*, and why do we even feel the need to question how it came to

be anyway? Who cares… let's just enjoy it while we can! The second man thought this answer wholly inadequate. He concluded that somehow cosmic forces of time and nature over probably billions of years must have somehow fused together and somehow caused a *Big Bang*, which then somehow produced energy and primitive life forms, all of which must have then somehow evolved to bring into being the magnificent city that we see before us today! Basically, he concluded that it came about somehow by chance, being the result of countless zillion, trillion, billion, millions of tiny random accidents over eons of time! But the third man thought this answer also wholly inadequate. Instead he surmised that the sheer beauty, the intricate design and perfect balance; and the way everything works and fits so perfectly together is evidence or proof of a Creator; of divine intelligence: God created the city.

Tony Holland, Professor of Chemical Engineering at the University of Salford, was a scientific humanist up to the age of thirty. Then he was challenged by the question, *'Is there a God?'* He concluded: *'On consideration, it was inconceivable to me that the complex system of which we are apart could have occurred without a creator. Just as a great symphony testifies to the skill of the composer, the world and the universe testify to the wisdom and power of God. Science is but a description of God's work.'*[5]

Dr Wernher von Braun was the first director of NASA's Marshall Space Flight Centre and was known as the 'father of the American space programme.' In a letter written to the California state Board of Education in 1972 Braun stated:

'One cannot be exposed to the law and order of the universe without concluding that there must be a design and purpose behind it all (…) The better we understand the intricacies of the universe and all its harbours, the more reason we have found to marvel at the inherent design upon which it is based. (…) To be forced to believe only one conclusion — that everything in the universe happened by chance —

would violate the very objectivity of science itself. Certainly there are those who argue that the universe evolved out of a random process, but what random process could produce the brains of a man or the system of the human eye? Some people say that science has been unable to prove the existence of a Designer. (…) They challenge science to prove the existence of God. But must we really light a candle to see the sun? Many men who are intelligent and of good faith say they cannot visualise a Designer. Well, can a physicist visualise an electron? (…) What strange rationale makes some physicists accept the inconceivable electron as real, while refusing to accept the reality of a Designer on the grounds that they cannot conceive him?'

Russian cosmonaut, Yuri Gagarin was the first man in space. He reportedly said from orbit: *'I don't see any God up here.'* Someone later pointed out that he would have done if he'd opened the hatch!

Professor Edwin Conklin, biologist at Princeton University, made this statement: *'The probability of life originating from accident is comparable to the probability of an Unabridged Dictionary resulting from an explosion in a printing factory.'*[6]

And Isaac Newton, the eminent 17th-century English physicist and mathematician famous for discovering the law of gravity, said, *'In the absence of any other proof, the thumb alone would convince me of God's existence.'* On one occasion, to assist him in his studies Newton constructed a model of the solar system which he placed in his office. Sometime later a friend and fellow scientist, who was an atheist, visited Newton and he marvelled at the model and asked who made it. *'Nobody!'* replied Newton. When his friend objected and charged him with being ridiculous, Newton asked him, *'If you accept that a model needs a maker, why do you have a problem when confronted with the actual universe?'*

As I said earlier, the Bible never tries to prove that God exists, it just assumes it. The opening sentence of the Bible, in full, reads: *'In the beginning God created the heavens and the earth.'*

I have been checking out some facts… The heavens or this vast galaxy that we live in, is spinning at the incredible speed of 490,000 miles an hour (136 miles a second), and yet, even at this breakneck speed, our galaxy still needs 200 million years to make one rotation. It's also been estimated that there are over one billion other galaxies just like ours in the universe, and some scientists say that the number of stars in creation is equal to all the grains of sand on all the beaches of the world! And yet, this complex sea of spinning stars functions with remarkable order and efficiency, so much so, that today, with human technological advancement, we can now send a man to the moon and predict with pin-point accuracy the exact time and place of his landing. All of these scientific facts support the biblical truth that order and creation are by design, and not somehow by chance or accident! [7]

The Old Testament prophet Isaiah wrote: '*Lift your eyes and look to the heavens: Who created all these? He who brings out the starry host one by one, and calls them each by name. Because of his great power and mighty strength, not one of them is missing*' (Isaiah 40:6). And the psalmist wrote: '*The earth is the LORD'S and everything in it, the world, and all who live in it; for he founded it upon the seas and established it upon the waters*' (Psalm 24:1–2). God created the world and everything in it: He is the Founder and Sustainer who holds all things together. The world and the universe are evidence pointing to God's existence. In St Paul's letter to the church in Rome he wrote, '*Since the creation of the world God's invisible qualities – his eternal power and divine nature – have been clearly seen*' (Romans 1:20). Paul says that all of creation is a signpost pointing clearly to God who made it.

The second pointer we can use to prove the existence of God is the fact of our morality, values and conscience. Here are some further truths that we can share to plant the seeds of the gospel, and further questions we can ask to provoke the thoughts of those who are receptive and seeking:

Evidence No.2: The Argument From Human Life And Personality.

A philosopher once voiced this opinion about the life of man. *'Man is Nothing; but fat enough for seven bars of soap, iron enough for one medium sized nail, sugar enough to fill seven cups of tea, lime enough to whitewash one chicken coop, phosphorous enough to tip 2200 matches, magnesium enough for one dose of salts, potash enough to explode one toy crane, and sulphur enough to rid one dog of fleas!'* Now, surely there must be more to life than this! Are we simply nothing more than a piece of protoplasm; a complex mix of chemicals, minerals and compounds; a chance coming together of raw inorganic matter?

Consider for a moment that a Grand Piano made by skilful hands has 240 strings on which beautiful melodies can be played. The tiny human ear, in comparison, has the equivalent of 24,000 strings, which enable us to hear those melodies. Consider that a closed circuit television camera has some 60,000 electrical photographic components, which pick up images and enable the camera to 'view' the surrounding area. In contrast, the human eye has over 137 million similar elements. Likewise, a personal computer has several hundred feet of wiring and the capacity to store several billion pieces of information. A man's brain, on the other hand, is infinitely more powerful. In fact, it has been suggested that the capacity for our brain to process and store information is, literally, unlimited. I once heard an Oxford professor on the television say that if you unravelled a man's brain cells and placed them end to end, there would be enough to go around the world twenty five times! There is no question about it, Man is a remarkably complex design and a wonderful creation as, indeed, are all of God's creatures... but Man is different from every other creature; mankind is uniquely distinct; special. Why?

The Bible tells us that God created man is his own image… male and female he created them. We are special because we are made in the image and likeness of God, who created mankind to have dominion and to take care of the earth – with God, but under God's direction. And because we are made in God's image we have been endowed with a personality and character and freewill, the ability to choose for ourselves. But we chose wrong; we chose to ignore God and to do things our own way, and we messed up… that's the problem – what the Bible calls sin – that separates us from God! But, coming back to our evidence: if we are simply the product of evolution, a chance coming together of raw inorganic matter, how can we ever explain our personality? Can a river run higher than its original source? No, (not unless it is manipulated by human engineering). Then how do we account for human personality? It is impossible for a river to run higher than its original source, and it is also impossible for inorganic matter to evolve into rational, thinking, calculating, emotional, human beings with individual character and personality. The fact is our personality points to God, who made us in His image.

Why do we feel generosity and gratitude when things go well; why do we feel the need to share and thank someone? On the other hand, why, in a crisis or when things go wrong, do we feel the need to pray or to cry out for help? Why do we claim *'it's not fair'*? Where does our concept of right and wrong come from, or our concept of fairness? If we are simply a product of chance, evolution or survival of the fittest, why then do we even care about morality and fairness? Where does our sense of justice come from? Our moral understanding, our values and sense of right and wrong all point to the existence of God, as does our conscience. Our conscience is an indicator to the existence of God if ever there was one!

Conscience is our God-given homing device, acting like a built-in moral code or inner-law within each and every one of us. Conscience is like an inner-judge who approves when we act and do what is right and disapproves when we act and do what is wrong (cf. Romans 2:15). And conscience has been described as a window that lets the light in: 'God's law or rule is the light, and the cleaner the window is the more light shines in. But if the window gets dirty and isn't cleaned properly, then the light grows dimmer until finally the light is shut out altogether and it becomes utter darkness. Our conscience instinctively makes judgments, sometimes acquitting us (we have a clear conscience) sometimes condemning us (we feel guilty). And this presence of an inner-law suggests that there must be a Lawgiver. Our conscience is a clear pointer to a God who is so concerned with right and wrong that He placed a homing device and a moral indicator inside each and every one of us.'

I wonder if you have ever watched The Simpsons on the television. In one episode Homer Simpson says, *'Dear Lord, the gods have been good to me. As an offering, I present these milk and cookies. If you wish me to eat them instead, please give me no sign whatsoever.'* (Then there's a brief pause.) *'Thy biding will be done,'* says Homer and the he promptly scoffs the lot! Homer Simpson thinks that God is absent, silent, impotent maybe… but that is definitely not the experience of millions and millions of Christians around the world.

Let me tell you about John Newton who was born in London nearly 300 years ago. His father was the commander of a merchant ship and as a boy John went to sea with him often. By the age of nineteen he had joined the navy but in the course of time he left and went on to captain his own ship, which he then plied exclusively in the slave trade.

On March 10th, 1748, whilst on a return journey from Africa with his ship fully laden with hundreds of slaves, Newton almost lost everything, including his own life. His ship was caught up in a violent storm and in a desperate bid to save himself, his ship, his cargo and his crew, Newton cried out to God to have mercy on him. God answered his prayers: The storm miraculously broke; everything was saved and the incredible events of that day changed John Newton's life forever.

As a direct result of this experience, Newton gave up his life as a slave-trader and, instead, he dedicated his life to serving God. He went on to become an ordained minister in the Church of England and he also became very close friends with John Wesley (founder of the Methodist church) and also William Wilberforce, the man who went on to lead the campaign for the abolition of slavery. John Newton, the once notorious slave trader turned Christian minister, dedicated the rest of his life to serving God and to serving others. He also wrote many wonderful hymns, one of the most famous of which is this one: Amazing grace, how sweet the sound: That saved a wretch like me; I once was lost, but now am found; Was blind, but now I see.

The words of this hymn capture something of the experience of millions and millions of Christians around the world: people who were once spiritually blind, but who now see who Jesus is. And this leads us to our third pointer and the most powerful argument we can use to prove the reality of God's existence...

Evidence No.3: The Fact of Jesus Christ.

In planting the seeds for the gospel, sooner or later we need to explain to people that the best and most conclusive way to discover if God really exists is to look at the time when God himself is said to have come to earth as a man, in the person of Jesus Christ, because then we have something tangible and concrete to investigate. The question that we need to pose (and help to answer) is this: *'Did Jesus Christ actually exist? If he did – and when you look at the historical and factual evidence you will know that he did – then you will also know that God exists.'* Here, then, are some further truths we can share to help plant the seeds of the gospel and provoke the thoughts of those who are receptive or seeking:

First, let me tell you the story about the man who lost his footing and fell over the edge of a cliff. As he slipped over the side he managed to grab hold of the root a tree.

Filled with panic, he called out, *'Help! Is there anyone up there?'* A powerful voice came from out of the sky, *'Yes, what do you want?'* The man pleaded, *'I fell over the cliff and am holding on to a branch for dear life. Please can you help me?'* The voice from above said, *'Do you have faith and believe in God?'* And the man replied, *'Yes, I have faith and I believe in God.'* The voice said, *'Then, let go of the branch and I will catch you!'* There was an anxious pause, and then the man yelled out, *'Is there anyone else up there?'* The point is it's one thing looking at the evidence with people to help them find answers it's another for them to come to trust in those answers. That takes faith, and faith is a gift that only God can give (cf. Ephesians 2:8). Our part is simply to be faithful in pointing people towards Jesus.

All four Gospel writers were absolutely convinced that Jesus was God's unique Son – so convinced they were willing to die to uphold that conviction. Mark opened his Gospel with the words: 'The beginning of the gospel about Jesus Christ, the Son of God' (Mark 1:1). And he concluded with the words of the Roman centurion at Jesus' crucifixion saying, 'Surely this man was the Son of God' (Mark 15:39). All of the apostles, including Paul and all the other New Testament writers were all of them equally convinced. Indeed, the New Testament is full of first hand witness statements, testimonies and eyewitness accounts about Jesus. As Michael Green points out: 'Jesus' contemporaries… came to the unshakable conclusion that he was the visible expression of the invisible God. His character, his teaching, his influence, his claims, his death, his resurrection all support that conviction. God, for who there are so many pointers [came to be with us so that we might come back to being with Him]!' [8]

But it's not just the writings of the Bible that attest to the fact that Jesus existed. As author and evangelist John Chapman pointed out: Josephus, a Jewish historian (and not a Christian), gives us further information in two of his literary works – *Antiquities of the Jews* (AD 93) and *Jewish Wars* (AD 75). In these works, we meet many of the people mentioned in the New Testament: Pilate, Annas, Caiaphas, Herod and others. Josephus tells us about John the Baptist as well as Jesus. He tells us that Jesus was a 'doer of marvellous deeds, a teacher of men who received truth with pleasure. He won over many Jews and also many Greeks.' He goes on to speak of Jesus' death and resurrection and of the group called Christians who came into existence because of him.[9]

When people investigate the person of Jesus they come to realise that the one thing that cannot be said about Him, is that Jesus was just another religious leader or a good moral teacher. He never meant to leave that option open to us. C. S. Lewis wrote in *Mere Christianity*:

> 'I am trying here to prevent anyone saying the really foolish thing that people often say about Him: 'I'm ready to accept Jesus as a great moral teacher, but I don't accept his claim to be God.' That is the one thing we must not say. A man who was merely a man and said the sort of things that Jesus said would not be a great moral teacher. He would either be a lunatic – on a level with the man who says he is a poached egg – or else he would be the Devil of Hell. You must make your choice. Either this man was, and is, the Son of God: or else a madman or something worse. You can shut Him up for a fool, you can spit at Him and kill Him as a demon; or you can fall at His feet and call Him Lord and God. But let us not come with any patronising nonsense about His being a great human teacher. He has not left that open to us. He did not intend to.'[10]

The fact is Jesus made many unique claims. Here are just a few of them taken from John's gospel: '*I am the bread of life. He who comes to me will never go hungry, and he who believes in me will never be thirsty*' (6:35). '*I am the living bread that came down from heaven. If anyone eats of this bread, he will live forever*' (6:51). '*I am the light of the world. Whoever follows me will never walk in darkness, but will have the light of life*' (8:12). '*I am from above... I am not of this world. I told you that you would die in your sins; if you do not believe that I am the one I claim to be'* (8:23–24). *'I am the gate for the sheep. (10:7)… whoever enters through me will be saved'* (10:v9). *'I am the good shepherd. The good shepherd lays down his life for the sheep'* (10:11). *'I am God's Son'* (10:36). *'I am the resurrection and the life. He who believes in me will live, even though he dies; and whoever lives and believes in me will never die'* (11:25). *'I am the way and the truth and the life. No one comes to the Father except through me'* (14:6).

Jesus, not only made unique claims, He also lived a unique life: a perfect life without sin and in full obedience to God. He taught with divine authority and amazed people with miraculous signs and wonders. Again, the New Testament is full of eyewitness accounts and testimonies of the disciples who witnessed Jesus perform wonderful miracles. Miracles of physical healing; from curing a fever, to leprosy, to the lame being able to walk and people who were blind being given back their sight. They saw miracles of spiritual healing, with all sorts of demons and evil spirits being cast out. Miracles over nature, such as turning water into wine, the feeding of thousands of people, Jesus walking on water and even controlling the weather, in calming the storm. And they even witnessed Jesus raising the dead with Jairus' daughter, the widow's son and Lazarus. All of Jesus' teachings and miracles are evidence pointing to the existence of God, but we need to explain to people that Jesus did not come to answer the question, *'how can I know there's a God'*: Jesus came to show us the way back to God… so that we can be forgiven and come to know God personally.

If we are to be successful fishermen, catching fish and keeping them, we need to explain the gospel to people (more on this in the next chapter, Evangelism: *The Message*). We need to explain that Jesus came to pay the price for our rebellion; for our ignoring God and choosing to live life our own way, what the Bible calls sin. We need to explain that Jesus came to die in our place, taking the punishment that we deserve; He came to offer himself as a perfect sacrifice, taking our sin upon himself at the cross; paying the price for our sin so that we wouldn't have to. And we need to explain that as a result of what Jesus has accomplished and done for us, forgiveness and eternal life are promised to all who will receive Him. Freedom from the burdens of guilt, wonderful new life and a restored relationship with God are a free gift to all who will receive it: to all who repent, accept Christ and follow him.

Some people go through life ignorant and unaware of the relevance of Jesus. I'm convinced this is because they have never really bothered or taken the time to really explore Christianity and discover for themselves, who Jesus is and what he came to do. This is astonishing, really, especially when you consider that the whole of the world records time as either before or after Jesus' death! How more relevant does a person have to be? Phillips Brooks was an Anglican Bishop who lived over a hundred year ago; he summed up the effect of Jesus' life like this:

'He was born in an obscure village, the child of a peasant woman. He grew up in still another village, where he worked in a carpenter shop until he was thirty. Then for three years he was an itinerant preacher. He never wrote a book. He never held an office. He never had a family or owned a house. He didn't go to college. He never visited a big city. He never travelled two hundred miles from the place where he was born. He did none of the things one usually associates with greatness. He had no credentials but himself. He was only thirty-three when the tide of public opinion turned against him. His friends ran away. He was turned over to his enemies and went through the mockery of a trial. He was nailed to a cross between two thieves. While he was dying, his executioners gambled for his clothing, the only property he had on earth. When he was dead he was laid in a borrowed grave through the pity of a friend. [Twenty] centuries have come and gone, and today he is the central figure of the human race and the leader of mankind's progress. All the armies that ever marched, all the navies that ever sailed, all the parliaments that ever sat, all the kings that ever reigned, put together, have not effected the life of man on this earth as much as that one solitary life.'

Many people ask the question, *'How can I know there is a God?'* and in this chapter we have seen that there is a great deal of evidence or proof for God's existence. When faced with this evidence people then have a choice to make. I sometimes say to people: 'Like the three men pondering over who built the city, each of us is faced with a choice: you can ignore the facts, shrug your shoulders and carry on with life as if it doesn't matter. You can deny the facts and say God is just an illusion; we are all an accident; a product somehow of chance. Or, if you really want to find out *'How you can know God'*… you can accept the facts, turn to Christ and receive forgiveness and eternal life. Then you'll really begin to live and know what life here, and in the hereafter, is truly all about. It's your call!'

Group Exercise: Most people love to talk about themselves, and God has made us curious, so let's be asking questions, challenging preconceptions and arousing curiosity so that people will want to hear more. Here are some good questions to ask (you might be able to think of others):

- Do you suppose that maybe what's going on in your life right now might be a sign, you know, like a God-thing to try and get your attention? What do you think?
- Have you got a faith? (How did that come about?)
- Let me ask you, what do you understand the Christian message to be all about?
- Is there anything about Jesus you find difficult to like?
- What are your views on the big questions of life: Who am I? Why am I here? And what happens when we die?
- Can I pray for you? This often takes people aback but they rarely say no.

Chapter 3

Evangelism: *The Message*

John 3:16 is the whole of the gospel message in a sentence:
'For God so loved the world that he gave his one and only Son, that whoever believes in him shall not perish but have eternal life.'

The word *evangelism* is derived from the Greek term meaning 'gospel' or 'good news'. Often the various forms of the word can cause confusion so allow me to explain it like this: To evangelise is to gospel – to gossip the gospel or spread the good news; an evangelist is a gospeller; an evangelical is a gospel centred person; and evangelism is the process or act of gospelling.

There is no getting away from the fact that evangelism today is extremely challenging. The UK, and indeed the whole of western society as a whole, is becoming more and more secular and as a result many 'traditional' Christian countries, including our own, have seen a steady decline in church attendance over a number of years. It has been rightly said that our society makes disciples far more effectively today than does the church! But thankfully, it is not all bad news here in the UK and there are still pockets of renewal and continued church growth, chiefly amongst evangelical churches (such as Holy Trinity, Brompton, famous for creating the Alpha Course) and also the mostly black Pentecostal churches, especially in London (with over 500 new churches in the London boroughs in the last 10 years. One of the largest, Kingsway International, has 10,000 Christians meeting every Sunday). But on the whole Christianity and church attendance is in decline in this country. Indeed, as I write this, the results of the 2011 census for England and Wales have just been published and from a Christian viewpoint, they do not make for positive reading.

The population of England and Wales in 2011 is stated as 56.1 million; a very sizeable increase of 3.7 million over the 2001 census, (which is mostly due to immigration). However, there is a big fall in the number of people who said they consider themselves to be Christian, and numbers dropped by a huge 4.1 million over the previous decade – from 37.3 million in 2001, to 33.2 million in 2011. In percentage terms, in England and Wales in the 2001 census, a substantial 72% of the population considered themselves to be Christian (albeit nominally) but this figure dropped to 59% in 2011. These are still big numbers, representing more than half the population declaring themselves to be 'Christian' (which at least shows an openness), but the reality is these figures bear no resemblance to actual church attendance figures. It is commonly thought that a great many people tick the box on the census form as being Christian because they are patriotic and rally to the flags of St George and St David, wanting to show themselves as being British and therefore 'Christian', rather than Muslim or Hindu or something else. Still, the decline in numbers is alarming, and the rate of decline is unprecedented. Something needs to be done. The wake-up call for the church to become more actively involved again in evangelism is urgent, and it's growing more and more so.

Indeed, the effect of secularism in our society is that a growing number of people now have very little knowledge of even the basic facts of Christianity. A reality that I have seen borne out time and time again in my role as an ordained minister, and especially in my undertaking numerous preparation classes with couples wanting their children to be baptised or wanting to get married in 'church'. It is extremely sad but true that many people today, who would nominally call themselves Christian, have little or no understanding of the Christian gospel, and they may never have even opened a copy of the New Testament. The situation seems to me rather like going back in time to the book of Acts where, for the most part, knowledge of the gospel was either extremely limited or completely non-existent. What we need is another Pentecost.

In the book of Acts, the New Testament church came into being through the outpouring of the Holy Spirit at Pentecost, and this outpouring resulted in the believers being empowered to witness and evangelise. (Evangelism and the Holy Spirit was discussed in Chapter 1.) There is no actual strategy, however, in the book of Acts or anywhere else in New Testament for evangelism. That's because the New Testament letters were written to churches and evangelism is the work of individual believers, and not churches per se. Personal, word-of-mouth evangelism (whether spoken or written) is the way that God chooses to draw people to Himself, including us (if we are Christians): we are those who have heard and responded. And because personal evangelism is just that, personal to each individual, there is no right or wrong way to do evangelism. The crucial thing is that we (individual believers and the church) seek to proclaim and spread the gospel. How else will the church grow? How else will our loved ones, our neighbours, friends and work colleagues be saved? We need to pray for the lost, we need to love them – love the hell out of them – but especially, we need to witness to them and tell them about Jesus (not leave them guessing).

In Romans, chapter 10 Paul talks of his desire to see his fellow Jews accept Christ, and in v13 he states: *'Everyone who calls on the name of the Lord will be saved.'* Then, in the next verse (v14), Paul goes on to pose a number of penetrating questions: *'How, then, can they call on the one they have not believed in? And how can they believe in the one whom they have not heard? And how can they hear without someone preaching to them?'* How indeed? How can the church grow; how can people today believe and come to faith in Christ; how can they *call on the name of the Lord and be saved* if they don't actually hear the gospel proclaimed; if we don't evangelise?

Evangelism is key. Without evangelism Christianity could, potentially, die out in just one generation. We need to tell people about Jesus – just as we were told about Him – and we need to tell them in a way that is culturally and contextually relevant.

In the Church of England, the *Preface to the Declaration of Assent*, which all Church of England ministers make at their licensing, states: *'The Church (...) professes the faith uniquely revealed in the Holy Scriptures and set forth in the catholic creeds, which faith the Church is called upon to proclaim afresh in each generation.'*[11] But what exactly is *the faith uniquely revealed in the Holy Scriptures and set forth in the catholic creeds* ('catholic' here means universal)? For the sake of clarity, it is faith in Christ for the forgiveness of sins? It is *'to repent and believe the good news!'*[12] That's why Jesus came, to show us the way of salvation, which is good news indeed. Jesus said, *'The Son of Man came to seek and save what was lost.'*[13] This is Christ's mission statement: *'To seek and save that which was lost.'* It is a mission that Christ began and one that He commanded his Apostles and the Church to continue with the divine directive to go and do likewise, to *'go and make disciples'* (the main verb here is *make*; we are to go and *make disciples* not wait around for would-be disciples to come to us). It is the directive known as *The Great Commission* and it's also wonderfully incarnational, in that, in going to *make disciples* we incarnate Christ: Christ dwells in us and promises to be with us always:

> *'Then Jesus came to them and said, "All authority in heaven and on earth has been given to me. Therefore go and make disciples of all nations, baptising them in the name of the Father and of the Son and of the Holy Spirit, and teaching them to obey everything I have commanded you. And surely I am with you always to the very end of the age."'* (Matthew 28:19–20).

God is a missionary, and He chooses to use us in His work of salvation, to seek and save the lost. It is sometimes said that witnessing is the gospel without words but evangelism is a conversation. That may be splitting hairs, but the message of the gospel needs to be clear and people need to understand that through Jesus the bad news has become good news. Evangelism is the proclamation of the message of Jesus. It is not something we do to people it is something we do for people, under the inspiration of the Holy Spirit. We are to proclaim the gospel afresh in each generation, that's our job, and the Holy Spirit – who is *The Evangelist* – is the one who convicts and converts people: that's His job. If we are going to be obedient and play our part properly, then we need to step out in faith and engage in empowered personal evangelism. That's what this book is all about.

Question then: If evangelism is the proclamation of the message of Jesus, how do we actually go about explaining the content of the gospel? To answer that question, I want to look at the very first Christian sermon, which was preached by the apostle Peter and was so effective that around three thousand people were converted and joined the church (cf Acts 2v41)!

In Acts Chapter 2, at Pentecost, after Peter and the other disciples had been filled with the Holy Spirit, they found themselves standing before a bewildered crowd, who had gathered because they heard a sound described 'like the blowing of a violent wind' and they witnessed the believers declaring the wonders of God in their own languages (foreign tongues they had not learned). So Peter, who was never shy to take advantage of an evangelistic opportunity, stood up and preached the first ever Christian sermon in which he shared the gospel, basically saying: *'Christ has died: Christ is risen: Christ will come again.'*

People are attracted to the gospel for various reasons but mostly people come to Christ because they are seeking meaning and purpose in life, or through curiosity, conviction or crisis, but always there must be conviction before there can be true conversion. The gospel really is simple, but far too many of us fumble over what to say, or get side-tracked or confused and start talking… well, mostly waffle, or else deep theological 'jargon' about original sin, man's fall from grace, penal substitution, atonement, justification and being saved by grace! Jesus never did that. One of the clearest proclamations of the gospel that Jesus ever gave is found in Mark Chapter 1v15, where Jesus said: *'The time has come. The kingdom of God is near. Repent and believe the good news.'* In other words, 'turn your life around; stop living life *your way* and instead live your life *God's way*. Confess your sin and repent of it. Accept Jesus, believe on Him and receive forgiveness, restoration and new life.' The gospel really is simple.

> **Practical Tip:** Here is an easy-to-remember evangelistic tool: It's really a simple four-word structure or skeleton to help us explain and share the Christian message with others. The four words are: **God, Man, Christ, Response.** And the message we need to convey is this: *God loves us. We messed up. Christ paid for it. We must receive him.* If you remember the structure, **God, Man, Christ, Response**, the rest is just adding meat to the bones!

So let's have a look together at Peter's sermon in Acts chapter 2 and as we do we will see Peter tackle these same four points – God, Man, Christ, Response – and at the same time he also tackles these questions: Who is Jesus? Why did He die? Why did God raise Jesus from the dead? Where is He now? And what does all this mean, for us? (This is the message we need to share with others.)

Who is Jesus?

'*Men of Israel, listen to this: Jesus of Nazareth was a man accredited by God to you by miracles, wonders and signs, which God did among you through him, as you yourselves know.*' (Acts 2:22) Many people accept that Jesus was a holy man, a religious leader or a good moral teacher. Indeed, He was all of those things but He was also far more than that. God accredited and endorsed Jesus' ministry with miracles, wonders and signs but who was He? Paul Little in his book, *Know What You Believe*, provides some clues with an orderly summary of some of the things that Jesus said about himself:

- Jesus claimed deity for himself in a way quite clear to his listeners. He said on one occasion, '*I and the Father are one*' (John 10:30).

- The high priest expressly asked Christ, *'Tell us if you are the Christ, the Son of God.' Jesus answered, 'Yes, it is as you say'* (Matthew 26:63–64).
- He announced for all to hear that, God [was] his own Father, making himself equal with God (John 5:18).
- He said he had authority to forgive sins (Mark 2:10).
- He said he would come on the clouds of heaven and sit at the right hand of the Mighty One (Mark 14:62).
- Implying authority to judge men, he said: *'The Father judges no one, but has entrusted all judgement to the Son'* (John 5:22).
- Several times Jesus asserted that he himself had the authority and power to raise the dead (cf John 6:39–40, 54; 10:17–18).
- He claimed omnipotence (all power) with the bold words *'All authority in heaven and earth has been given to me'* (Matthew 28:18).
- During his life he demonstrated power over nature by stilling the stormy waves (Mark 4:39) and turning water into wine (John 2:7–11).
- He also demonstrated his power over physical disease (Mark 3:10), power over demons (Luke 4:35) and power over death by raising Lazarus from the grave (John 11:43–44).
- Ephesians 1:19–21 describes his *'incomparably great power in the heavenly realms, far above all rule and authority; power and dominion'*.
- In a conversation with some who were against him, Jesus remarked that Abraham rejoiced to see his coming. The Jews were dumbfounded: *'You are not yet fifty years old… and you have seen Abraham?'* He replied, *'I tell you the truth, before Abraham was born, I am!'* (John 8:57–58). Of course He existed before Abraham since He was the Creator (who created Abraham!)
- Jesus was able to challenge his enemies with the question, *'Can any of you prove me guilty of sin?'* (John 8:46).
- He frequently said at a point of crisis, *'My time has not yet come'* (John 2:4, 7:6). Then finally he said, *'The hour has come for the Son of Man to be glorified'* (John 12:23). A little later, as he contemplated the awfulness of the cross, he said, *'Now my heart*

is troubled, and what shall I say? "Father, save me from this hour?"' (John 12:27) No, the reason Jesus had come, as He said, was to *'seek and to save what was lost'* (Luke 19:10) and to *'give his life as a ransom for many'* (Mark 10:45).

- Jesus Christ accepted worship due only to God. After his resurrection He commended rather than rebuked doubting Thomas who fell at his feet and declared with awe, *'My Lord and my God!'* (John 20:28).[14]

All that Jesus said about himself, and all of his teachings and miracles are evidence or signs pointing to who He really is. Who is He? God's anointed Messiah, the Christ, *'a man accredited by God to you by miracles, wonders and signs,'* says Peter (in Acts 2:22).

Why did Jesus Die?

'This man was handed over to you by God's set purpose and foreknowledge; and you, with the help of wicked men, put him to death by nailing him to the cross.' (Acts 2:23)

Amazingly, mankind's wicked act of rejection is also God's divine act of salvation. Jesus' offering of himself as a willing sacrifice, and His death on the cross, was all part of God's set purpose and foreknowledge. God was behind it all but we still remain responsible for it all!

I read an account some time ago about a little girl who was suffering from a rare and serious disease. Her only chance of recovery appeared to be a blood transfusion from her five-year old brother, who had thankfully survived the same disease and had developed the antibodies needed to combat the illness. The doctor explained the situation to her little brother and asked the boy if he would be willing to give his blood to save his sister. He hesitated for a moment, then he took a deep breath and said, *'Yes, I'll do it if it will save her.'*

As the transfusion progressed he lay in a bed next to his sister and smiled, seeing the colour returning to her cheeks. Then his face grew pale and his smile faded. He looked up at the doctor and asked with a trembling voice, '*Will I start to die straight away?*' You see, being so young, the little boy had misunderstood the doctor: He thought he was going to have to give his sister all his blood!

In a sense that's what Jesus did for us. Each one of us has a serious disease – it's called sin! Each one of us needs to be saved and Jesus is the one who saves us, because He has paid the price with his own blood. This is the gospel, the good news of salvation: Jesus saves us when we accept that his blood pays for our sins. At the end of the day all sin has to be paid for but God in His wonderful grace and mercy has provided us a choice: We can accept Jesus and He pays for our sin, for free, or people can reject Jesus and they pay for their sin themselves, but then they have hell to pay!

Jesus was born a man because he had to die as a man, on behalf of all mankind. Jesus acted as our substitute. He came to die in our place, to offer himself as a perfect sacrifice on our behalf, taking our sin upon himself at the cross. Why did Jesus die? To pay the price for our sin so that we wouldn't have to.

There is a story told about a pastor in America who introduced a visiting speaker to his church, and an elderly preacher walked up to the pulpit and told this story: 'A father took his son and his son's best friend on a sailing trip when a storm overturned the boat sweeping them all into the ocean. The father managed to scramble up onto the upturned hull and grabbing the life buoy and rope he had to make the most painful decision of his life – which boy to throw the lifeline to and which one to sacrifice. He knew that his son had accepted Christ but his best friend hadn't. In anguish the father yelled, '*I love you son,*' and threw the rope to his son's friend. By the time he'd hauled the boy back to the capsized boat; his son had disappeared beneath the waves. His body was never recovered. The father knew that his son would step into eternity with Jesus but he couldn't bear the thought of his friend facing eternity without Christ.' At the end of the service a teenager approached the old man and said, *'That's a nice story, but what father in his right mind would sacrifice his son's life in the hope that the other boy would become a Christian?'* – *'You've got the point,'* the old preacher replied. *'But I'm standing here today to tell you, that story gives me a glimpse into what it must have been like for God to sacrifice His only Son for us. And I also understand you see, because I was that father, and your pastor... he was my son's best friend!'*[15] Let me say it again: Jesus died to pay the price for our sin so that we wouldn't have to.

Why did God Raise Jesus from the Dead?

'But God raised him from the dead, freeing him from the agony of death, because it was impossible for death to keep its hold on him.' (Acts 2:24)

But God raised him from the dead... we love a beautiful 'but' don't we? Pun intended! (Don't worry; God has a sense of humour.) Even so, the words *'but God'* are two of the most important words in the whole of the Bible: *But God raised him from the dead.* Why? Because it was impossible for death to keep its hold on him. Jesus' resurrection from the dead demonstrates His power to defeat satan... *death could not keep its hold on him.*

Here's a bit of theology for us: Romans 6:23 says: *'The wages of sin is death, but the gift of God is eternal life in Christ Jesus our Lord.'* This Scripture is clear: the wages or penalty for sin is death. Many of us are already aware and understand this but let's take the reasoning a step further: If death is the penalty for sin, then when Jesus (a sinless man) dies, God (if He is fair and just, which He is) will not punish or make the sinless man pay with death, and so He is bound to be raised from the dead. It's inevitable: *death could not keep its hold on him…But God raised him from the dead.*

Jesus' resurrection is also God's affirmation or *'yes'* to the sacrifice that Jesus made being accepted. That's why Jesus didn't stay dead? His resurrection is the absolute proof that Jesus' sacrifice is all-sufficient for the forgiveness of sins, and its proof too, that all believers will inherit eternal life, just as Jesus promised. Think about it: If Jesus had remained dead, how would we ever know we are forgiven? If there was no resurrection then there is no forgiveness… if there is no resurrection there is also no judgement, no punishment and no reward; no heaven! If there is no resurrection then this life is all there is! *But* (again, we love a beautiful 'but' don't we)… *But* there is life after death; the resurrection is true and the evidence for it is overwhelming.

Former Lord Chief Justice of England, Lord Darling, said of the resurrection, *'In its favour as a living truth there exists such overwhelming evidence, positive and negative, factual and circumstantial, that no intelligent jury in the world could fail to bring in a verdict that the resurrection story is true.'*

'God has raised this Jesus to life, and we are all witnesses of the fact,' said Peter (in Acts 2:32), with all the other disciples stood beside him (as witnesses). And we also know that God raised Jesus to life because the entire New Testament bears witness to His resurrection, and the Church only began because of the resurrection. The Church stands and falls on this one truth! So, if Jesus has risen….

Where is Jesus now?

Peter answers that question in Acts 2v33: *'Exalted to the right hand of God, he has received from the Father the promised Holy Spirit and has poured out what you now see and hear.'* Jesus has been glorified and exalted to the right hand of God where He now reigns and waits for the Second Coming. It's brilliant: Jesus has no longer limited himself to one physical human body in order for us to meet with Him. Now, He has poured out the Holy Spirit on all believers, and today Jesus is just as real with us spiritually as he ever was physically.

Again, if there was no resurrection there was no Pentecost. But the outpouring of the Holy Spirit on believers – the Spirit we have within us – is proof that Jesus is alive. Christ *has* died but Christ *is* risen and Christ *will* come again. (Interesting, that the verb *'pour out'* (in Acts 2:33) illustrates that God's gift of the Holy Spirit is neither a drizzle nor a shower but a pouring out; a downpour! God wants us to be completely saturated in the Spirit, so that we pour out the Holy Spirit to others.

So... What does this all Mean?

Peter concluded in Acts 2v36: *'Therefore let all Israel be assured of this: God has made this Jesus, whom you crucified, both Lord and Christ.'* Jesus is both Lord and Christ, in whom lies all the authority of heaven and earth.

So what did all this mean to those who heard Peter's evangelistic message, and what does it mean to us today? Peter later wrote in his epistle (1 Peter 3v18): *'For Christ died for sins once for all, the righteous for the unrighteous, to bring you to God.'* The message of the gospel brings people to God and presents them with an opportunity to respond: either they accept the gospel or they reject it (or put off making a decision, which is still rejecting it). After the first-ever Christian sermon the people questioned Peter and the other disciples saying: *'What shall we do?'* And Peter replied (v38): *'Repent and be baptised, every one of you, in the name of Jesus Christ for the forgiveness of your sins.'* People need to recognise who Jesus is and what He has done for them, and they also need to know how to respond to the gospel (we will be looking at this in the next chapter).

Some young lads, led by Johnny, were always making fun of an old man, tormenting him and calling him names because of the way he hobbled as he walked. *'Here comes old Rattlebones,'* they'd call out, teasing him whenever they saw him on the street.

Then one day there was a knock at Johnny's door and his mother went to answer it. There, standing on the doorstep was Old Rattlebones himself. *'My goodness it's you!'* cried Johnny's mother with obvious delight. *'Please come in, come in'* she beckoned him. *'Johnny, come downstairs quickly,'* shouted his mother, *'come and meet the man who once saved your life.'*

Johnny appeared instantly on the landing, but then he froze when he recognized who it was: Looking up at him his mother said, *'Remember I told you how, when you were a baby, your pram rolled down the hill and fell through the ice into the canal? This man here, with no regard for his own personal safety, jumped in the icy waters to rescue you, but then he got stuck himself.'* Then pausing slightly, she continued, *'He saved your life that day, but the prolonged exposure to the icy waters left his body so severely damaged that he has suffered from chronic arthritis ever since!'*

Overcome with guilt and shame for the way he had ill-treated and ignored his rescuer, Johnny looked at the man who had risked all to save him. *'Please forgive me,'* he said, *'I had no idea who you were. I didn't know it was you!'*

Our forgiveness was terribly costly for Christ, but gloriously free for us... People need to recognise who Jesus is and what He has done for them, and they also need to know how to respond.

The gospel really is simple to understand, so simple that it is often offensive... some people think they need to earn God's favour and forgiveness; they need to do something – be charitable, give to the poor, help the needy, make sure that your good deeds outweigh your bad, try to keep the Ten Commandments and so on (all of these are good and proper and they please God, but none of them can earn God's forgiveness). There is nothing that we can ever do to add to the finished work of the cross. Jesus has already done everything that is necessary for our sins to be forgiven and for us to become children of God. As someone once said: '*Trying to earn God's forgiveness or favour, or trying to add something to what Jesus has already accomplished, is like trying to improve a Monet painting by adding some brushstrokes of your own! However much care we take, we won't be able to add to the masterpiece but in fact, we will actually deface it and destroy it.*'

The gospel *really* is simple to understand... God made it simple because *God doesn't want anyone to perish, but everyone to come to repentance* (cf. 2 Peter 3:9). We need to explain to people that in order to receive God's forgiveness, God's favour and God's promise of the Holy Spirit, they need to repent and be baptised in the name of Jesus. It is simple to understand but it is not so simple to do! We have to turn away from our sin and through faith accept Jesus as our Lord and Saviour.

Again, the crucial thing is that individual believers and the church seek to proclaim and spread the gospel. How else will the church grow? How else will our loved ones, our neighbours, our friends and work colleagues be saved? We need to pray for the lost, we need to love them – love the hell out of them – and especially, we need to evangelise and tell them about Jesus (not leave them guessing). We're in the world for a reason: we're in it to win it. Let's do what we can to spread the gospel and share the good news of Christ. We need to be willing to take a risk and to have a go but remember it's not about the size of the seed you sow; it's all about God who can make it grow.

> **Personal Exercise:** Ask a non-Christian friend if they would be willing to help you by listening to you explain the Christian message. Just be honest. Tell them you have been reading this book about evangelism and one of things

you have been asked to do, one of the challenges, is to give a short explanation of the Christian message to someone, and ask for their feedback. When you have explained the gospel ask which parts were clear or unclear? This exercise provides a great opportunity for asking spiritual questions and it also allows you to practice and refine your efforts.

Take action on the above exercise straight away otherwise it will drop off the radar. Pray and ask God to lead you to someone to 'practice' on. Take time to be still and wait on God to respond; don't try to think up names by yourself – maybe *So-and-So* or *Thing-a-ma-Jig* – just wait on the Lord to lay someone on your heart. Then pray some more and go practice.

Group Exercise: Strike a match (or allow 60 seconds on a stopwatch). Turn to your neighbour and tell them the gospel before you burn your fingers! (Swap) How did you get on?

- Remember to be clear about the gospel requirements (repent and believe) and don't dilute or misrepresent the message.
- Remember the four gospel words: God – Man – Christ – Response. (God loves us. We blew it. Christ paid for it. We must receive him.)
- Use an intriguing opening statement such as: *'I believe in heaven and I believe in hell and I believe the only difference between those two places is Jesus.'*

On the following pages I have included four gospel illustrations, which you might find useful in sharing the message and good news of Jesus with others.

A gospel illustration using two chairs as props:

(1) When God created us God and mankind were together: Personal relationship

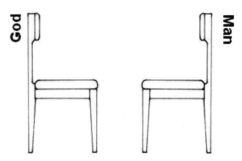

2) But the world rebelled and turned its back on God: We rejected Him

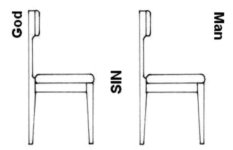

(3) Because of our sin God must sadly turn his back on us:

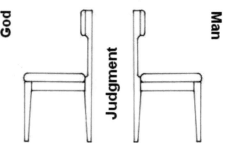

(4) But through Jesus death on the cross, God is now able to forgive sinful people:

(5) All that remains is for sinners to repent, accept Jesus and to turn back to God to receive forgiveness:

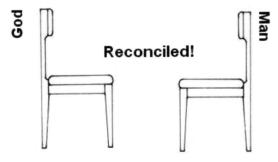

The Five-Second Gospel created by Judson Poling

God's Message:
> 'God loves us,
>> we blew it,
>>> Christ paid for it,
>>>> we must receive him.'

The Four Key Characters:

Character 1: God. 'God loves us.'

• God is **loving**.

God is love. Whoever lives in love lives in God and God in him (1 John 4:16b).

• God is **holy**.

And they were calling to one another: *'Holy, holy, holy is the LORD Almighty; the whole earth is full of his glory'* (Isaiah 6:3)

• God is **just**.

The LORD is known by his justice (Psalm 9: 16a)

Character 2: Us. 'We blew it.'

• Humans were originally created good, but we became **sinful**.

For all have sinned and fall short of the glory of God (Romans 3:23)

• We deserve **death**.

For the wages of sin is death (Romans 6:23a)

• We are spiritually **helpless**.

All of us have become like one who is unclean, and all our righteous acts are like filthy rags (Isaiah 64:6a)

Character 3: Christ. 'Christ paid for it.'

* Christ is **God**, who also became man.

  Christ Jesus: Who being in very nature God, [was] made in human likeness (Philippians 2:5b–7b).

* Christ died as our **substitute**.

  For Christ died for sins once for all, the righteous for the unrighteous, to you to God (1 Peter 3:18a).

* Christ offers his forgiveness as a **gift**.

  For it is by grace you have been saved, through faith — and this not from yourselves, it is the gift of God — not by works, so that no one can boast (Ephesians 2:8–9).

Character 4: You. 'We must receive him.'

* We must **respond**.

  Yet to all who received him, to those who believed in his name, he gave the right to become children of God (John 1:12)

* We receive him by asking Christ to be our **forgiver and leader**.

  If we confess our sins, he is faithful and just and will forgive us our sins a purify us from all unrighteousness (John 1:9)

  But in your hearts set apart Christ as Lord (Peter 3:15a).

* The result of receiving him is our spiritual **transformation** by the Holy Spirit.

  What this means is that those who become Christians become new persons. They are not the same anymore, for the old life is gone. A new life begun! (2 Corinthians 5:17, NLT).

Source: Becoming A Contagious Christian: Participants Guide 2007, Mittleberg, Strobel & Hybels, Michican: Zondervan, p.66–7.)

The Roman Road[16]

Use this illustration with people who are open to looking at the Bible and considering its claims for themselves. Some people need to see the gospel explained in black and white in the Bible, and this is a good way to do that. Each verse in the illustration (all taken from the book of Romans, hence the name) is followed by possible dialogue you may have with your friend.

Romans 3:23
For all have sinned and fall short of the glory of God.

The Bible tells us that all have fallen short. That certainly includes me. Would you agree that it also includes you?

Romans 5:8
But God demonstrates his own love for us in this: While we were still sinners Christ died for us.

Here is the whole of the gospel in a sentence. Romans 5:8 tell us:

- That God loves us and wants us to be in relationship with him.
- We are sinners who need to be rescued/forgiven before we can be reconciled, before we can enjoy a relationship with God.
- We can't grant our own forgiveness or rescue ourselves, nor can we do anything to earn our own salvation… so God does it for us.
- God sent his Son to die in our place and take away our sin. That's how much he loves us; how he demonstrates his love for us.

Romans 6:23
For the wages of sin is death, but the gift of God is eternal life in Christ Jesus our Lord.

We both just admitted that we have fallen short. This verse shows we are in a real predicament, because *the wages of sin is death.* In other words, this is what we have earned as a result of falling short.

The good news comes out in the second half of the verse. We do not have to suffer death on account of our sins, because *the gift of God is eternal life in Christ Jesus our Lord.* But it is not enough to just know this — we have to act.

Romans 10:9–10

If you confess with your mouth, 'Jesus is Lord,' and believe in your heart that God raised him from the dead, you will be saved. For it is with your heart that you believe and are justified, and it is with your mouth that you confess and are saved.

Jesus said, in Matthew's Gospel (1:15): 'The time has come. The kingdom of God is near. Repent and believe the good news!'

Romans 10:13

Everyone who calls on the name of the Lord will be saved.

This verse shows that if we are willing to call on the name of the Lord, to accept Jesus as our forgiver and leader, then we will be saved.

Would you like to take this step?

Tip: Mark these verses in a small NT and 'chain' them together. In the margin next to Romans 3:23, write 'Romans 5:8,' which will show where the next milestone in the road is. (Next to 5:8 write 6:23. Next to 6:23 write 10:9–10. Next to 10:9–10 write 10:13.) Keep this NT in reach for whenever you need it.

The Heart of the Gospel

Martin Luther called John 3:16 'the heart of the Bible – the Gospel in miniature.' It is so simple that a child can understand it; yet it condenses the deep and marvellous truths of redemption into these few pungent words:

- 'God'...The greatest Lover
- 'So loved'...The greatest degree
- 'The world'...The greatest number
- 'That He gave'...The greatest act
- 'His only begotten Son'...The greatest gift
- 'That whosoever'...The greatest invitation
- 'Believeth'...The greatest simplicity
- 'In Him'...The greatest Person
- 'Should not perish'...The greatest deliverance
- 'But'...The greatest difference
- 'Have'...The greatest certainty
- 'Everlasting Life'...The greatest possession [17]

Chapter 4

Evangelism: *The Response*

In response Jesus declared, 'I tell you the truth, no-one can see the kingdom of God unless he is born again.' John 3v3

Evangelism is a process not an event. As I write this opening sentence I am mindful of a man I have just made friends with and who has agreed to join an explorers course that I am due to run shortly at our church. (We call the course Just Looking at Christianity.) The man's wife is a committed Christian and a member of the church, and she told me recently: 'Ian, it's just wonderful that he wants to come on your explorer's course. I've been praying for my husband for 20 years!' (From the conversations I have already had with him I can see the Holy Spirit is at work and I am hopeful and confident that this man will make his own response to Jesus in due course.) Let me say it again, evangelism is a process not an event, and in the case of my new friend, it was his wife who helped to begin the process some 20 years ago.

It is really important we grasp that evangelism is a process and not an event, because understanding this saves us from much discouragement and despondency when things don't work out as quickly as we might like. Having said that, the overall aim of evangelism is always to win converts and make disciples, and so sooner or later the proclamation of the gospel must lead to an invitation, which, in and of itself, demands a response. In fact, effective evangelism always demands a response; at least that's where evangelism is heading, maybe not immediately but ultimately, towards a response; seeking a decision for Christ.

Repeating what I said earlier, to evangelise is to gossip the gospel, to spread the good news; it is the proclamation of the message of Jesus with an appeal or call to action. This is what we see happening in the New Testament, especially in the book of Acts, where there is a proclamation of the gospel followed by an appeal or call to respond. Take, for example, Peter addressing the crowds in Acts Chapter 2: first comes the proclamation (v32): *'God has raised this Jesus to life, and we are all witnesses of the fact,'* and then the appeal or call to respond (v38): *'Repent and be baptised, every one of you, in the name of Jesus Christ for the forgiveness of your sins. And you will receive the gift of the Holy Spirit.'* The appeal or call is to *repent and be baptised*; and the promise *is the gift of the Holy Spirit* to all who respond; that is, to all who respond in faith. Let's take a brief look at what it means to repent, to be baptised, and to receive the Holy Spirit.

Firstly, repentance: It is imperative that we understand and explain to others the difference between being sorry or remorseful for things that we have done wrong and being repentant – which is not the same thing. When my children were growing up and they committed some minor misdemeanour and were sorry for what they had done, I would often say to them: *'It's good that you are sorry but I don't want so much to hear sorry as to see sorry.'* In other words, its right to be remorseful and apologise but to change your wrongful behaviour, that's what really matters! To be remorseful is to be sorry. Judas Iscariot, who betrayed Jesus, was full of remorse. In fact, he felt so sorry for himself, and was so full of guilt for what he'd done, that he went out and hanged himself. But as far as we know Judas didn't repent; he didn't seek forgiveness and restoration; he didn't seek to live a changed life that honours Christ. He was remorseful, yes, but not repentant (cf Matthew 26:24–25, 27:3–5 and John 17:12). To be remorseful is to be sorry but to repent is far more than just being sorry: to repent is to confess your sins, your wrongdoing, and to seek God's forgiveness; to repent is to want to turn your life around;

to turn away from your old way of life and to seek to live a new life through the Lord Jesus. – Jesus calls us all repent… and then to keep on repenting when we know we have sinned.

Secondly, baptism: All believers should be linked to Jesus through baptism. If you are a believer and follower of Christ and you haven't been baptised then you really should be baptised, publicly. Not because this is some kind of ritual or ceremony that we need to do in order to be saved (salvation is by faith alone: cf Ephesians 2:8–9), but because Jesus instructed us to do it, because we need to be obedient and because it helps to edify and build up the church. (It's a great reminder and a real encouragement for believers to see people publicly affirming their faith.) The water of baptism symbolises the washing away of sin and our being forgiven and made clean by turning to Christ. In full immersion baptism the candidate goes down under the water, which symbolises darkness, separation, dying to the old self, and then they are symbolically raised to live a new life, washed clean and forgiven in Christ. More than that, though, baptism is a sacrament ordained by Christ himself. According to *The Book of Common Prayer* baptism is: *'An outward and visible sign of an inward and spiritual grace given unto us, ordained by Christ himself, as a means whereby we receive the same, and a pledge to assure us thereof.'*[18] In other words, baptism is a sign or symbol that represents our acceptance of God's grace to us in Christ and God's acceptance of us through Christ. In the *Institutes of the Christian Religion* Calvin explained it like this: *'Circumcision was for the Jews their first entry into the church, because it was a token to them by which they were assured of adoption as the people and household of God, (…) In a like manner, we also are consecrated to God through baptism, to be reckoned as his people.'*[19] All believers should be linked to Jesus through baptism. Again, Acts 2:38 says: *'Repent and be baptised, every one of you, in the name of Jesus Christ for the forgiveness of your sins. And you will receive the gift of the Holy Spirit.'*

Thirdly, then, let's look at receiving the gift of the Holy Spirit, which is a part of God's salvation gift pack we get when we first become a Christian. Jesus said to his followers: *'you will receive power when the Holy Spirit comes on you; and you will be my witnesses'* (Acts 1:8). The Holy Spirit empowers us to be witnesses for Jesus (as we saw in Chapter 1), but more than this, the Holy Spirit – who is also sometimes called, 'Sanctifier of the people of God' – is given to change us; to make us holy (set apart) and to help us live our new life in Christ. The Bible teaches that God is love (1 John 4:8), that is, it's God's nature to love, and so He continues to love us, even with all our failures and flaws. Think of it like this: A painting, even a damaged one, is worth millions if it was created by a great artist. All people, even damaged ones, are created in the image of God and are so valuable and of such worth that God gave up his Son for each one of us. The fact is, if you were the only person in the whole world Jesus would still have gone to the cross just for you. That's how much He cares about you; that's how much He loves each and every one of us. One author wrote, *'If God had a refrigerator, your picture would be on it. If He had a wallet, your photo would be in it. He sends you flowers every spring and a sunrise every morning. Whenever you want to talk, He'll listen. He can live anywhere in the universe, but He has chosen your heart. And what about the Christmas gift He sent you at Bethlehem? Not to mention that Good Friday at Calvary. Face it, He's crazy about you!'* God is love and God loves us just the way we, but He loves us too much to allow us to stay the way we are. We are like a stone with a flawed diamond in it! And God wants to free the diamond in each one of us, so that we shine and radiate His glory. God wants to grind away the flaws and polish us to perfection and so that's one of the things the Holy Spirit does. The Holy Spirit is like God's engagement ring, His pledge of heaven given to us while we are still on earth. The Holy Spirit is our constant companion (He is never further than a thought away); He accompanies us on our daily walk; He is our comforter and our Counsellor; He blesses us with His presence and peace; He helps us to worship; He encourages us; He comforts us; He teaches us; He strengthens us… and He also convicts us of sin and leads us in the way of repentance, again and again, so that we can keep on receiving forgiveness and restoration, again and again, as we go through life and the refining process known as sanctification; that is, the life long process of being sanctified, being made holy and growing in the likeness of Christ.

> Let me share an illustration using an imaginary glove: If this glove (this is where your imagination comes in!) represents our body, or a temple, you'll see that in and by itself it is empty, pointless and lifeless. It might look nice in appearance but if the glove is not used for the purpose for which it was created, it is ineffective and useless. When we accept Jesus and become a Christian the Holy Spirit comes to live within us. The Holy Spirit is like my hand that fills the glove and now the glove is full of life, and it's useful and can fulfil the purpose for which it was created... to glorify God.

Christians are like a house or a temple where God lives by the Holy Spirit. But even so, we can still quash the Spirit, we can ignore Him, we can treat Him as an occasional visitor rather than the owner-occupier. We can even live in the same house and hardly ever see each other or communicate. Friends, that's not what Jesus wants for any of us. The Holy Spirit is given as a gift. And God intended for the gift (and gifts) of the Holy Spirit to be extremely active in believer's lives, communicating God's will and purposes to us, so that we might live lives that praise, honour and glorify God. Nicky Gumbel, pioneer of the hugely successful *Alpha* course, maintains that all Christians should be completely overwhelmed by, immersed in and plunged into the Spirit of God. He likens the experience to sometimes being like a hard dry sponge dropped into water. There can be a hardness in our lives, which stops us absorbing the Spirit of God. It may take some time for the initial hardness to wear off and for the sponge to be filled. You see, it's one thing for the sponge to be in the water (baptised), it's quite another for the water to be in the sponge (filled with the Holy Spirit). But when the sponge *is* filled the water literally pours out from it.[20] It is the same with a Spirit filled Christian; the presence of God literally flows out from them.

So the appeal or call is to repent and be baptised; and the promise is the gift of the Holy Spirit to all who respond… that is, to all who respond in faith. Unfortunately, however, it has to be said that many people today (churchgoers!) mistakenly depend on their baptism or in sharing the Lord's Supper (the Eucharist or Holy Communion) for their salvation. Sadly, I know from personal experience several people like this, and it's painful and frustrating to observe. However, I have to say that I have also known several others, personally – folk who have been coming to church for years – and who then finally 'get it' and make a commitment to Christ. As a preacher and evangelist this always gives me hope.

A few years ago when I was studying at theological college I did a three-month church placement (work experience) at St Sebastian's Church in Wokingham as part of my training for ministry. (Subsequently I went back to 'Saint Sebs' after Theological College to serve my curacy). On the very last Sunday morning of my placement I was allowed to preach an overtly evangelistic sermon, at the end of which I made an appeal to accept Christ. It was a wonderful moment. Around twenty people stood to pray a prayer of commitment and give their lives to Jesus. One of them was my stepmother, Jean (who this book is dedicated to). It has been an absolute delight to watch Jean's faith grow over the years since then, and to see so many answers to prayer. She has also become a great encouragement to me. As I write this Jean is currently accompanying two of her friends on a Christianity Explored course at her church. She not only invited her friends to come along to the course, she brought them along and stayed with them.

The sad thing is there are many people who come to church and think they are following Christ but in reality their actions, or lack of them, tell a different story. They practice Churchianity not Christianity. It's all head knowledge and not heart knowledge and the fact is, they are missing out on salvation by a foot (that's

12 inches — the distance between the head and the heart). Do you remember the story of the rich young ruler in Luke 18: He came to Jesus and said, 'What must I do to be saved?' Even the way he asked the question implies that he imagined he could obtain salvation the way he had acquired everything else — through his own efforts. He mistakenly thought salvation was just a deed or a payment away, but it's not and it never can be. As someone once said, 'Only a cold-hearted God would sell salvation to those who can afford it. Salvation costs more than we can ever afford. That's why we don't need a résumé, we need a redeemer.' We can't come to God demanding fairness or justice, we can only come seeking His grace and pleading his mercy. Christianity, true Christianity, is not about rules, robes, rituals or reverends, it's about a relationship. (Religious traditions can be helpful or hurtful, depending on how we use them.) Again, true Christianity is not a religion it's a relationship; it's not about intellectual head knowledge it's about heart knowledge; it's not about religious rule keeping or doing things in a certain way (even though tradition is valuable and can be very important), it's about our love for Christ expressed in willing obedience, and not simply going through the motions.

When my daughter, Kimberley, was at college she worked part-time as a cashier at a local convenience store. One day a very excited lady came into the shop waving her lottery ticket in the air and exclaiming that she'd won the lottery big time! Apparently she had picked 5 or 6 of the numbers correctly and knew she'd won a substantial amount — the jackpot was £9.2 million, as I recall — and she came into the shop to check how much she had won and to see if there were any other winners. Everyone crowded around as Kimberley took the winning ticket and processed it in the Lottery Machine to register the win and see how much the winnings actually were. What happened next can only be described as the biggest look of shock on someone's face that you have ever seen in your life! It transpired that the woman had indeed picked the winning numbers but for the wrong day of the week: she had picked to play the Lotto on the

Wednesday, instead of Saturday's draw! This lady came into the store absolutely convinced that she had won the prize but when the truth was revealed she left humiliated and distraught. Terribly sad!

Jesus said that's how it will be for some people on the last day. They'll say, *'But Lord, Lord, it's me, don't you recognise me?'* And He will say to them, *'Away from me, you evildoers! I never knew you'* (cf Matthew 7:21–23). These are the folk that practice Churchianity, not Christianity. It seems there will be folk who talk the talk, who perform religious duties and even do good works (miraculous good works!), and yet their hearts and motives aren't right. It seems they are more interested in self; in personal position, prestige, plaudits or power maybe, because Jesus will say to them, *'I never knew you'* – and that really is the key: Jesus doesn't know them and they don't know Him, not personally. There's no personal relationship and so Jesus calls them, *'evildoers'* (unrepentant sinners)... *away from me. I never knew you... you didn't let go; you didn't fully surrender to me. Calling me Lord and my being your Lord are two separate things. I never knew you because you didn't die to self, you didn't let go and fully give yourself to me.'*

Have you ever experienced a situation when you have been excluded from a place where you thought you had the right to enter? A few years ago at Gatwick Airport my family and I were refused permission to board our holiday flight to the Canary Islands even though we had paid for our tickets and had seat reservations. I won't reveal the name of carrier (who is no longer trading anyway) but on this charter flight they had deliberately oversold the seats, rather than turn business away. My family and I queued up at the airport check-in desk for about an hour (it was really slow) and just as we were getting to the front of the queue they closed the check-in saying the flight was now full, and leaving about twenty-five bewildered passengers stranded, all of us with tickets! Our reserved seats had simply been given to someone else who was in the queue before us. (Eventually, the tour operator did put us on another flight, but it was about 4 hours later and all our on-going transport at the other end had been messed up!) We thought our seats were guaranteed: surely, if you have a confirmed ticket, you ought to be allowed to board the aircraft, no matter where you are in the queue! It was all so unfair and unreasonable.

In Luke 13:22–30 Jesus teaches about us entering into the kingdom of God through the narrow door before it is too late, because one day soon the door will be closed and no further admittance or entry will be allowed. Jesus warned us that there are some who think they are saved when really they are not! These are the people, Jesus says, who once the door is shut will come knocking and pleading to be let in, claiming some association or knowledge of Christ, but it's too late and they will not be allowed entrance. Now some people may think Jesus' warning in this passage is unreasonable and unfair: saying that the owner of the house will only let people in up to a certain point in time and then he will shut the door in the faces of any other people, and no matter how much they plead to be let in, he will refuse saying, *'he never knew them so their claim for entry is not valid!'* Far from being unreasonable, though, Jesus, as we shall see, is actually *warning us* not to be those who miss out on the feast. Allow me to explain (it may be useful to read the passage first, Luke 13:22–30):

As Jesus made his way to Jerusalem – his final destination – someone asked him (v23), *'Lord, are only a few going to be saved?'* But Jesus doesn't answer, at least not directly. As NT Wright explains in one of his commentaries, 'Jesus simply won't be drawn on giving numbers or statistics to satisfy human inquisitiveness.'[21] (Jesus came to steer us towards repentance and faith, not to gratify our curiosity.) And so to paraphrase the question, someone asked him, *'Lord, will the saved be few?'* and Jesus, in effect, replies: *'wrong question my friend; rather will the saved be you?'*

You see, instead of answering the question directly Jesus challenges his listeners (v24), *'Make every effort to enter through the narrow door, because many, I tell you, will try to enter and will not be able to.'* So what exactly is this narrow door? There are several passages in the New Testament where Jesus is referred to as the gate, the way or the door. For example in Matthew 7v7 Jesus says: *'Ask and it will be given to you; seek and you will find; knock and the door will be opened to you.'* In John 10v9, *'I am the gate'* (or in the English Standard Version)... *'I am the door. If anyone enters by me, he will be saved...'* And in Revelation 3v20 Jesus says: *'Here I am! I stand at the door and knock. If anyone hears my voice and opens the door, I will come in and eat with him, and he with me.'* So what does it mean to make every effort to enter through the narrow door? In a nutshell, it is our earnestly desiring to know Jesus, and diligently striving, that is, making every effort to follow him whatever the cost, because the reward is (and will be) *so* worth the effort.

On the subject of effort and reward: I understand that on average it takes 250 tons of rock to produce a single diamond. And each diamond, once it's been refined, is then sorted into 1 of 5000 different categories, based on the carat, colour, clarity and the cut of the precious gemstones. Now that's an awful lot of effort for just one diamond but then, just look at how precious diamonds are! Jesus said we are to *make every effort to enter through the narrow door*. In other words, we should earnestly desire to know Jesus and diligently strive, that is, make every effort to follow him now whatever the cost because the reward is, and will be, worth so much more than we can ever imagine. The Bible tells us, *'No eye has seen, no ear has heard, no mind has conceived what God has prepared for those who love him'* (1 Corinthians 2v9). That's how wonderful it's going to be; so wonderful it's indescribable in earthly terms!

But Jesus also warned us not to put off making the decision because the narrow door (of opportunity) will not remain open forever. In fact, one day soon the door will close and then, as Jesus said, many will try to enter but it will be too late. They will not be able to enter because they didn't strive while they had the chance; they didn't make every effort to enter while the door of opportunity was still open... they were warned but they took no notice! Why does God warn us? Because he doesn't want anyone to perish but for everyone to come to repentance (cf 2 Peter 3v9): He warns us because he loves us.

Jesus also warns us there are some who think they are saved, when really they are not! These are the people, Jesus says, who once the door is shut, will come knocking and pleading to be let in, claiming some association or knowledge of Christ: They will say, *'We ate and drank with you, and you taught in our streets'* (v26): Today it might sound more like, *'we shared in the Eucharist or Holy Communion and listened to sermons and Bible teaching'* but these people aren't Christians; they are not committed to Christ: *'I don't know you or where you come from'*, says Jesus (v27). Again, that's the key: Jesus doesn't know them and they don't know Him. There is no relationship and so Jesus calls them, *'Evil doers... away from me.'* Like many of the Pharisees, these people are probably the respectable, religious, rule keepers and some of them, no doubt, regular churchgoers... but they don't really know the Lord Jesus and their hearts are not changed: They practice *Churchianity* not *Christianity:* They know about Jesus but they don't actually know him, personally. Oh, they may very well know about religious tradition; and protocol; and fairness; and charitable giving and so on, but they do not know the love of Christ or his forgiveness, which is all-of-life changing, and they have not accepted Christ into their hearts, and so Jesus calls them *'evildoers'*; people who knew something of Christ but who were not willing to repent and believe; they were not willing to turn away from their sins and receive Christ's forgiveness while they had the opportunity to do so.

Like many of the self-righteous Pharisees, there are also many today (in the church, on the fringes and outside the church) who are deluding themselves: they think their place in heaven is guaranteed but they are wrong, and they put little or no effort at all into discovering the truth. Jesus proclaims that one day they'll be sorry but by then it will be too late: and all the weeping, anguished grinding of teeth and pleading in the world won't change a thing, the door of opportunity will be closed. The case for the church to engage in evangelism is urgent. We need to try and reach lost people while there is still time... but how much time is there? No one knows the answer to that question!

Supposing we were to go into your local town centre and conduct a survey asking people this question: '*If you died tonight and you stood at the gates of heaven and God said, 'Why should I let you into my heaven?' how would you respond?*' In reality there are only two answers that question: one is the wrong answer and the other the right answer. The wrong answer basically adds up to any statement that says '*because of what I have done*'. For example, '*God, you should let me into heaven because...*'

- *I'm a kind and considerate person. I try to help others when I can and I often give to charities* (in other words, my good deeds).
- '*God, you should let me into heaven because...I've kept the 10 Commandments* (I've not killed anyone; I don't lie or steal or commit adultery.)
- *I'm a decent law-abiding citizen. I might not be perfect but if you balance things out, like on a pair of scales, I'm a fairly good person.*
- *I've read the Bible: maybe not all of it but some of it, and I pray quite often.* (That doesn't make you a Christian.)
- *Well, I've been baptised/confirmed and I regularly go to church and share in the bread and wine.* (That doesn't make you a Christian.)
- *I believe in Jesus* (so does the devil!)
- *And I grew up in a Christian home and my parents are Christian.* Great, but being born into a Christian family doesn't make you a Christian, any more than being born in a launderette makes you a washing machine! It is often said that God only has children, not grandchildren. In other words, tradition or family connections don't make a person a Christian, only a personal encounter with Jesus, and accepting Him as Lord does that.

We need to understand that God's standard is 100% perfection and by this standard everyone fails, so no one can ever be saved by good works, no matter how hard we try. If we could attain salvation through our own efforts then Jesus' death would have been absolutely pointless. It is only Jesus' death on the cross that makes us right with God. Jesus paid for our sin so that we wouldn't have to. That's why Jesus came… to show us how to enter the kingdom of God through repentance and faith. He came to show us the way to heaven and to rescue us or save us from hell (which is eternal separation from God).

The correct answer to the question: '*Why should I let you into heaven*' is this: '*God you should let me into heaven because of what Jesus has done for me!*' We are not saved because of anything we have done but because of what God has done for us in Christ. Again, Ephesians 2:8–9 is crystal clear: '*It is by grace you have been saved, through faith – and this not from yourselves, it is the gift of God, so that no one can boast.*' In short, the only thing that we have ever contributed to our salvation is our sin!

Question then: If we are not saved by our good works or by our own efforts, what does Jesus mean when he says (in Luke 13:24) that we should '*Make every effort to enter through the narrow door?*' '*Ian,*' you may ask, '*if we are saved by God's free gift of grace why do we even need to make any effort at all?*' Well, look again at Ephesians 2 and the following verse (v10), which says: *For we are God's workmanship, created in Christ Jesus to do good works, which God prepared in advance for us to do.* We are not saved by good works but for good works, which God has planned in advance for us to do. God has plans for us; there is kingdom work for us to do; good works – but our good works and our making every effort do not lead to our salvation, it's the other way around: our salvation, knowing that we are saved, leads to our good works. *Good works are the fruit of our salvation not the root of our salvation!*

You know, there will be lots of people we recognise in God's kingdom, but there will also be lots of surprises there too! There will be many there whom we would never have expected to see and there will be others who we would have expected but who aren't! To his Jewish audience Jesus said, *'the patriarchs and prophets will be there but you yourselves will be thrown out'* (cf Luke 13:28). They imagined as God's chosen people and with their special relationship, that they would be first in the kingdom, but Jesus said (v29): *'People will come from the east and west and from the north and south, and will take their places at the feast in the kingdom of God'*. People from all four corners of the world, from every nation, tribe, people and language: The gospel will be preached all over the world and people will respond and be saved and follow Jesus. That's what is happening all over the world right now. Let's be a part of it and let's make every effort to help as many people as we can to enter through the narrow door. In the final analysis, entry into the kingdom of God is not going to be about *who* you are and what you've done, but *whose* you are and what He has done for you! That is the ultimate question that demands a response: Who do you belong to? Whose are you?

Jesus won't take the throne of our lives by force. We have to invite Him to be King, and so I want to finish this section by offering a personal prayer of response that you can use with others (or indeed yourself, if you have not already done so). I want to make it clear, however, that it's not the actual words of a prayer that matter, so much as the heartfelt repentance and faith of the one who utters the prayer. That is the important thing. Take for example the criminal on the cross next to Jesus, the one who knew he was being justly punished and who sought to be made right with God; his words of response were simply this: 'Jesus, remember me when you come into your kingdom' (Luke 23:42). Again, it's not the actual words of a prayer that matters, but the heart of the one who prays. Jesus saw this man's repentant heart, and he saw his personal faith. The man acknowledged Jesus was the King (only a king has a kingdom), and so the Lord accepted his heartfelt prayer and He answered him (v43): 'I tell you the truth, today you will be with me in paradise.' By the grace of God this dying man entered into the kingdom through the narrow door before it closed on him... even if he did it by the skin of his teeth!

I don't ever recommend people playing with eternity and putting off making a response to the gospel. Besides, there are so many benefits to becoming a Christian now – it's not just pie in the sky when you die; there is also loads of meat on the plate while you wait (as we shall see in Chapter 6 when we look at *The Bible and Evangelism*). Here then is a recognised model of the prayer of repentance based around saying three things to God: sorry, thank you and please.

- Saying sorry to God for going your own way and for not treating him as your king.
- Saying thank you to God for sending Jesus to die so that you could be forgiven.
- Asking God to please forgive you, and help you to live with Jesus as your king.

PRAYER: Lord Jesus, I am sorry for living my life my way instead of your way (*mention anything in particular that is on your conscience*). Thank you that you gave your life on the cross for me. I want to give my life back to you now. Please forgive me and grant me the gift of the Holy Spirit. Come into my life and help me to change into the person you want me to be. Amen.

Group Exercise: Break into pairs or small groups. Read 2 Corinthians 4:1–6 together and then answer these two questions:
Q1. What is God's role in our evangelism and preaching the gospel?
Q2. What is our role?

Group Exercise (allow 5 minutes for this Bible study): What motivation does the New Testament give for us to evangelise. Break into small groups of 3's or 4's and see how many Scripture verses you can come up with that motivate us to evangelise.

Chapter 5

Evangelism: *And the Church*

And the Lord added to their number daily those who were being saved.
— Acts 2:47

The early Christian Church did not regard evangelism as an occasional activity, instead it was an integral part of everyday church life, and we see in the book of Acts that people were continually joining the church and more were being added to their number daily. The church, in our own generation, needs to get back this kind of expectation. Indeed, as the church around the world continues to grow it is estimated that the net increase in the number of Christians every single day worldwide is 70,000. People are continuing to be added to the church daily. It is still happening and in growing numbers but we need to pray and expect it to be also happening in our churches.

Evangelism is our ultimate act of worship. (Think about it.) If I were to ask you what your church is like I wonder how you would respond: Do you have sound biblical teaching and preaching? Do you have great music and worship? Is your church Spirit-filled and prayerful? Is it a friendly and welcoming family church? I hope it is all of these things because we need to go to church to be built up in our faith; to pray together; to worship and fellowship with other Christians, and so that we can be edified, encouraged, equipped, recharged and empowered... but for what reason: just so that we can feel good? No! We are meant to come in to church to receive nourishment for the soul and then we are meant to go out again… seeking continually to do our bit in fulfilling the great commission before Jesus returns – because then it will be too late: There will be no evangelism in heaven! The only reason Jesus has not yet returned can only mean that there are still yet more people who are going to be saved. Can you think of any other reason in Scripture to explain why Jesus has not yet come back? Just how many more people will be saved or how much longer before Christ returns, only God knows. The question is what will we do in the interim as we wait and work towards that Day? That's what I want to look at this section: what can we do, as church, to be more effective at reaching out and inviting others in.

The Church and the Christian community can be an extremely powerful witness to our non-Christian friends. People long to belong; they long to belong to a community that will accept them and care about them, and in this regard the local church is, or should be, in a league of its own.

Is your church a welcoming church? Most people I have asked this question to say *'yes'* or *'we try to be'*, and so then I ask them: *'And is it also an invitational church?'* You see, our churches can be very welcoming (which is great) but if we are not also inviting others to come to church, well then we are only welcoming ourselves each week, and then church quickly becomes a holy huddle! If your congregation is not inviting it doesn't matter how welcoming you are as a church! Mark Stibbe gives this advice to church leaders: *'We need to urge every member of the church to be intentional about inviting unbelievers to hear the gospel and about Jesus. You can have the most evangelistically potent church in the world, but if its members are not into inviting their friends, it's pointless. Individual members need to make evangelism a personal priority. This for me is the real key to church growth. We must prioritise evangelism.'*[22] As Christians we need to be welcoming outside of the church so that people warm to us as individuals, and we then need to be invitational; inviting people to come to a church service, or an event, or a meal, or to *Alpha* or *Christianity Explored*, and so on. In Matthew 4:19 Jesus went out to the Sea of Galilee to choose his first disciples: *'Come, follow me,'* Jesus said, *'and I will make you fishers of men.'* To follow is to fish! Fishers of men and women: that's what Jesus calls us to be. Fishers of men, not aquarium keepers! To be a fisher of men and women you have to go fishing, not wait for the fish to jump out of the water and into your lap! And, of course, to catch fish you have to go where the fish are. If we spend all of our time with other Christians then we won't ever be in a position to invite non-Christian people along to church. If people are going to be reached for Christ, then mostly it will happen through friendships, not strangers. So, if all our friends are Christians we need to get out more; we need to get out of the church building and meet more people. We are to fish and catch people for Christ: mostly, that means tickling the fish for a while – getting to know them, making them comfortable in our presence – not blowing them out of the water with a stick of dynamite! Note that Jesus said we are to fish for them, not hunt them down or shoot them! As fishers of men and women our job is to catch them. It is the Holy Spirit's job to clean them!

In Ephesians 4:11 we read that Jesus gave to the church some to be apostles, some to be prophets, some to be evangelists, some to be pastors and teachers… Christ gave to His church some to be *evangelists.* There are folk in our churches who are outgoing and sociable and *'natural'* evangelists: we need to encourage them and give them freedom to do what God has gifted them to do. Church leaders must not tie evangelists down. Eagles tied to a stake have no soar left in them! We must set the evangelists free to do what they have been gifted to do… mission not maintenance! But that must not become an excuse for everyone else to down tools and say I am not gifted in evangelism and so therefore I will leave that to someone else! Everyone can and should invite others to *come and see,* and this, in itself, is part of the evangelism process. Evangelism is not an option for the church; it is a command not a suggestion. Matthew 28:19 says: *'Go and make disciples of all nations.'* For Christ's sake, let's go! We are the ones who have to go out and bring the lost in. The church is not meant to be a cruise ship or a pleasure boat for the select few, it's meant to be a lifeboat and we are the crew, the rescue party. Evangelism is a body ministry and it very much should be all hands on deck! Who can you invite? Is God laying someone on your heart right now?

Now let me ask you another question: If you invite a friend to come with you to church and they decline or make some excuse, do you think God will be pleased with you for asking them? I have a friend who is also a business partner, Roy Maslin (we own property together). Roy testifies that before he became a Christian he always wanted to come to church but he just needed someone to invite him. Thankfully someone did. It is our job to invite people but only God can stir a person's heart to make them accept the invitation. It is only God who causes the church to grow; it's the Lord who adds people to the church – *'the Lord added to their number daily those who were being saved'* (Acts 2v47). Let's be clear about exactly what Jesus commands us to do: we are to *'go and make disciples'*, not wait for folk to come in to church and ask, *'Excuse me, how can I become a disciple of Jesus?'* We need to say to the church, for Christ's sake, let's get out of the boat! We are the ones who have to go out and bring the lost in. Again, the church is not meant to be a cruise ship but a lifeboat, and we are the crew, we are the rescue party. Evangelism is our responsibility. As someone has said, *'The response is to come from us, and the ability will come from God.'*

It is God who seeks the seeker and it is God who draws people to Jesus. Paul says in Romans 3:10–11 (quoting from Psalm 14): *'There is no one righteous, not even one; there is no one who understands, there is no one who seeks God.'* And in John, chapter 6 Jesus said: *'All the Father gives me will come to me (v37)... No one can come to me unless the Father who sent me draws him (v44)... Everyone who listens to the Father and learns from him comes to me (v45)... No-one can come to me unless the Father has enabled him'* (v65). According to these verses, people do not seek God on their own initiative. People do not come to Christ unless the Father draws them. People don't ask questions about spiritual matters unless God is at work in their lives. We need to discern where God is at work in other people's lives and then go and join Him. Again, don't pray, *'Lord, bless my work for you,'* pray, *'Lord, let me be a blessing where you are at work.'*

So why do we have to evangelise or invite people to come to church or an outreach event or an explorers course, and so on? If it is nothing to do with us and it is all down to the Father drawing people to Jesus, why do we need to evangelise and share the gospel? Why do we have to go out of our comfort zones to come alongside others and invite them to come and see? Of course, God is perfectly capable of doing this work himself, so why do we have to do it? The answer is because God chooses to reach people through people. Indeed, the wonder of it all is that God should choose to use people like us in the first place, to be His message bearers to draw others to himself. It's an amazing act of grace on God's part, and a wonderful privilege for us. Again, as Charles Spurgeon has said: 'To be a soul winner is the happiest thing in the world.'

Human beings are relational (just as God is relational), and it is through our efforts and personal evangelism that God draws others to Jesus. It's so very important that we grasp this: It is God who causes the church to grow but He chooses to use us in the process. So… if we are not being invitational it's like we are locking the door of our churches to those on the outside. If we are not being invitational then we are potentially stopping God from doing what he wants to do through us. We need to unlock the door of our churches, figuratively speaking, and open the way for God to do his work through us by inviting others to come and see… in fact, more than just invite people; we need to actually bring them with us. Yes, bring them! Put yourself in the other person's shoes for a moment. How intimidating do you think it would be to enter into a place of worship as a stranger, when you don't know anyone and you don't know any of the customs that happen inside? When we invite someone to attend church, they are much more likely to go if we go with them, and hold their hand so to speak. So we need to make it easy for guests to come and see… we should go and pick them up (or get them to come over to 'yours' beforehand).

Why is there so much apathy or reluctance amongst Christians, certainly here in the UK, to invite their friends to church? I think, to our shame, we (corporate we) have become too insular; we have become so busy and caught up with church business and affairs, that we have become anaesthetised to evangelism and what the church is really about and meant to do. Archbishop William Temple once said, '*The church is the only organisation that exists for the benefit of its non-members.*' Evangelism is our ultimate act of worship. Many in the Church have forgotten this. A little while ago I was at a lunch attended by several ministers from the surrounding area, representing maybe a dozen different churches. I asked them this question: '*If I were an unbeliever in your parish or community do you have an event that you could invite me to?*' I was hoping to glean some fresh ideas. No one answered, not a single minister, but there was plenty of navel gazing! (It was this very experience that first prompted me to think about writing this book.) What we need in our churches is revival, a new Pentecost (we will be looking at this subject in more detail in Chapter 7: *Prayer* and Evangelism).

People who spend a long time in prison often become institution-alised; they become so comfortable with their surroundings that they don't want things to change. The same also applies to those who are locked up in church culture! Here are some of the reasons why Christians don't invite others to church. They think:

- I am no good in this area; it's not my gift. I feel too uncomfortable.
- To be honest it is just not on my agenda: I'm too busy and never really think about it.
- I am quite a reserved person and my faith is a private thing. I don't like to talk to others about it.
- I am afraid of receiving a 'no' and being embarrassed.
- I don't have any non-Christian friends.
- I am not very happy with things at my church and so I don't want to invite others to come along.
- I have asked lots of people before but no one came, and so that has put me off.

- I am concerned that if they say yes and come along they won't enjoy the experience.
- I invited people before and they had a bad experience.
- You can never tell what the sermon is going to be like at my church… it can be really cringe!

What then can we do then as church members and leaders to encourage the flock to evangelise and to be invitational?

Firstly, all of these objections should be acknowledged and turned into teaching points to show people how to overcome their fears and inhibitions.

Secondly, we need to understand that… as the leader so is the church: If a church leader has a ministry for prayer and healing, so does the church; if a church leader has a ministry of the Word and for preaching, so does the church; if a church leader has a sacramental ministry so does the church, and so on and so forth. Church leaders, therefore, need to be invitational themselves in order to set an example for their congregations to follow.

Thirdly, we need to celebrate the invitation – the yes's and the no's. If we only acknowledge and celebrate successes then we cut off and discourage people from inviting others. We need to understand that sometimes it takes several no's before someone finally says yes. So, we should celebrate and honour the number of invitations not just the number of acceptances… sometimes it's just not the right time. The gestation period of a human baby, from the time of conception to birth is approximately 9 months (266 days/38 Weeks). In other words, we need to bear in mind that there is a time for sowing and a time for reaping, but they are not the same seasons.

There is a true story (the details of which, unfortunately, elude me) of a godly man who prayed for over thirty years that his best friend would find Christ and come to faith. The Christian man eventually died without seeing his prayers answered but a few days later, during the funeral service and after listening to the tributes and eulogy, his best friend was finally converted and gave his life to Christ! Throughout this book I have continually made the point the evangelism is a process and not an event.

Dr James Engel developed a model, known as the 'Engel Scale', that's very helpful in describing evangelism as the process leading towards a decision. Imagine a straight line or a scale with zero at the centre, and minus numbers to the left (−1, −3, −10 etc.) and positive numbers to the right. A person who is asking questions and seeking God could be said to be a −1 on the scale, there is a genuine desire but they are not quite there yet. And someone who wants to *knock your block off* rather than hear the gospel, well, they're a −10! Believers are all on the plus side… and as we continue to grow and mature in faith we move along the line (+1, +4, +10, etc.). I reckon I must be at least into treble figures by now! Seriously, if you move a person from say, −7 to −5, is that not part of the evangelism process? Absolutely, it is. You may not actually be there for the 'zero hour', but God has certainly used you in the process.

Fourthly, church leaders should teach their congregation that in being invitational the only thing you have to lose is the security of your comfort zone, but you have such a lot to gain: Your confidence will grow, so will your faith, God will be pleased with you, and your friend may just enjoy the experience and make real advancements on their own spiritual journey to find God.

Fifthly, church leaders should teach their congregation to nurture a deep and intimate relationship with God, and to shine for Jesus. There is something profoundly attractive and deeply compelling when we let the light of Jesus shine through us, when we radiate joy, and light, and life to others.

Sixthly, we need to remind our congregations that success breeds success: the more invitations we make the more positive responses we will get.

And seventhly, we need to encourage our congregations to build friendships with non-Christians and then introduce them to fellow Christians. The more contacts we have the more invitations (and repeat invitations) we are able to make. I once heard Bishop Andrew Proud say, 'Every church has a flock and a fringe. The secret to church growth is to feed the flock and foster the fringe, and seek to bring the two together as often as possible.' We need to ask ourselves how can we do this. In particular, the Church of England is the largest cell church in the land with tons of fringe contacts. Church leadership teams need to ask themselves how can we develop these contacts into relationships? Suffice for me to say here, that the church should be through the community like Blackpool is through a stick of rock!

Michael Harvey is one of the founders of the 'Back To Church Sunday' initiative and he travels extensively to speak at churches and training events on 'Unlocking the Growth' of our churches. I met him at a recent training seminar for church leaders where he offered us '12 simple steps to becoming an invitational church' and I share these with you below:

1. (Create vision): If every one of us invited a friend and they accepted we would double our congregation. Let's do it.
2. (Modelling): I, as a church leader, I am going to invite someone, will you?
3. (Cascading: the law of multiple returns): Make sure every member of the church has had a personal invitation to invite someone.
4. The gift of friendship: Teach about how God connects people through friendship.
5. The power of your story: remember who invited you.
6. Get every member to ask themselves the question: who has God been preparing in my life?
7. Practice the question: *would you like to come to church with me?*
8. Pray for courage to invite, and pray for those being invited.
9. Make the invitation.
10. Go and pick up your invited guest from their home.
11. Introduce them to your friends over food and coffee.
12. Assume they are coming the following time you meet as a church and invite them again. [23]

As I said earlier, the church and the Christian community can be a powerful witness to our non-Christian friends. People long to belong; they long to belong to a community that will accept them and care about them, and in this regard the local church is, or should be, in a league of its own. The question is, then, how can our churches become the sort of places that attract seekers? What sort of churches should we be like? To answer that, I want to look briefly at the effects of Pentecost on the newly Spirit-filled church in Jerusalem. This is what the first Christian church was like, and what church should still be like today. First, however, a little background into the story of the church and the unfolding events of church history.

Many people mistakenly think that the Day of Pentecost was the birthday of the church, but this is incorrect because the church, as the people of God, had already been around for at least four thousand years, going right the way back to the time when God chose Abraham (Genesis 12:1–3). The Day of Pentecost does not describe the *birth* of the church but the *continuation* of the church after the revelation of Christ: that is, the remnant of God's people became the Spirit-filled church or body of Christ. Actually, in many of our Bibles there is one page that really shouldn't be there, and that's the blank page that usually separates the Old Testament from the New. You see, there is no separation between the Old and the New Testaments: It's a continuation not a separation; it's not an old religion and a new religion; it's not an old church and a new church. The New Testament Church is a continuation of the Old; it is part two, if you like. (What we call the *Early Christian Church* is the beginning of part two… the end of the story.)

In fact, the Bible reads a bit like a whodunit in two parts. The Old Testament sets the scene: The crime is committed, evidence gathered, judgement passed and the penalty announced… but the Old Testament ends in a state of suspense, because there has been continuous talk – prophecy; of some kind of reprieve – of payment being made on behalf of the guilty, of a Messiah who would pay a ransom and rescue his people. But who… we are left in suspense! (Dun, Dun, Dun!) Cue: The New Testament; part two of the story, which tells us not only 'who-done-it' but 'who-done-it' so incredibly well, that not only was the ransom paid, but there is also a guarantee of forgiveness, restoration, renewal and eternal life available for free to all who accept and follow Jesus. The theme of the whole Bible from Genesis 12 (with the call of Abraham) to Revelation 22 (and the renewal of all things) is *how lost people can be found and rescued* – it's a search and rescue mission, and the main character in the story from beginning to end is the Lord Jesus Christ.

So let's now take a glimpse of God's vision for His church, as we look at the effects of Pentecost on the first Christian church in Jerusalem. Again, this is what the first Christian church was like, and what church should still be like today. As we are considering *'Evangelism and The Church'* I want us to look at Acts 2:42–47, which will give us an insight into what a living Spirit-filled church is called to be and to do – which should be both an encouragement and a challenge for us. Verse 42, in particular, is often regarded as laying down the four marks of church: teaching, fellowship, breaking of bread and prayer. The first Christian church was a learning church, a generous church, a worshipping church, and a praying church – *and the Lord added to their number daily those who were being saved.* Let's look at these 'four marks of church' in a bit more detail:

1. They were a learning church

(v42): *They devoted themselves to the apostles teaching.* According to v41, the Jerusalem church had grown by 3000 people overnight and these Christians (although they weren't actually called that until Acts 11:26) sat at the apostle's feet, eager to study and learn all they could. They knew that Jesus had given the apostles authority to teach and so the church devoted themselves to the apostles' teachings. We are still called to do this today, but the way we submit to apostolic authority and teaching is through the New Testament Scriptures, which we are told, are so powerful they can change people's lives… if they allow it to! Hebrews 4:13 says: *The word of God is living and active. Sharper than any double-edged sword, it penetrates even to dividing soul and spirit, joints and marrow; it judges the thoughts and attitudes of the heart.* God's word is dynamic and powerful, living and active.

The Bible is one of the main sources of nourishment for a Christian, which is why God gave it to us. If we want to know God more, if we want to love him and know his love for us more, then we really need to read and study our Bible, regularly, diligently. Not to read it as a tick box exercise, just going through the motions... because then the words just flow through our mind like water gushing through a pipe – nothing sticks! We need to read it thoughtfully, prayerfully, expectantly and regularly; daily. Now I am not into guilt-tripping people into doing something they don't want to do, but church leaders really should encourage their congregations to be reading the Word of God daily to find nourishment for the soul, and which will then change us from the inside out and make us more attractive for Christ... and more effective in evangelism.

Many people find regular reading of the Bible difficult. Someone said to me recently, *'I feel guilty for not reading it more than I do but when I do read it, I don't really get anything out of it.'* I can understand that, but it's a bit like being on a diet and after the first day saying, I don't feel any different so what's the point? I recommend people start by creating a habit of spending 15 minutes a day in reading and studying God's word, maybe just a chapter a day. Not to try and get through it but to try and see what to get out of it! Look for God on every page, then look for yourself on the same page and ask, how is this applicable to me today, what is God saying to me?

In running nurture courses or speaking to new believers I will often ask: What happens if we pray and pick up our Bible to read and meditate on it for, say, 15 minutes a day, and then we put the Bible down and because we're so busy we forget or we don't pick it up again for another week or more? What do you suppose happens? Well, frankly, nothing very much! It's like a drop in the ocean! Oh, the actual time spent happened but because it didn't keep on happening it had no real lasting effect. But the opposite is also true: It's like me adding a drop of blue food dye into a bucket of water. After adding one drop nothing much happens: after two or three drops – it's the same: but after three or four weeks of continually adding a drop, day after day, the water in the bucket starts to turn blue. Same with us: if we cultivate a daily habit of praying and reading God's Word, things may not change overnight, but very soon we will start to see a very marked and positive difference. We will become more 'colourful'… more Christ-like, and, ultimately, more effective in our evangelism!

2. The second mark of a living, Spirit-filled church is: they are a generous and sharing church.

They were devoted to each other and to their fellowship (v42) – they were a family: *'All the believers were together and had everything in common. Selling their possessions and goods, they gave to anyone as he had need* '(v44–45). These are challenging verses to us, but those early Christians really loved one another. They were a generous and sharing church: giving money, yes, but also sharing meals together and fellowship and caring for one another.

Warning: We need to also practice hospitality more within our congregations. There is a real danger that established friendships within the church can easily become cliques, where regulars appear friendly on the surface and they smile and speak to newcomers, but then they spend all of their time with a select group of friends and no one else is invited to join the group. We need to look for ways to include and involve newcomers. People come to church looking to find a place to belong and be loved and accepted, and if they don't find it they soon stop coming

Again, the first Christian churches were devoted to each other and to their fellowship – they were a family; they loved one another deeply and they were cheerful and willing givers, practicing hospitably and giving financially to support the work – and the Bible tells us that '*God loves a cheerful giver*' (2 Corinthians 9:7). God gives to us generously and willingly, not reluctantly, and God calls us to be conduits of his grace not cul-de-sacs! But our giving is not just about money, it is also about our time and how we use it; it's about being hospitable; it's about looking out for the needs of others; it's about our serving the local church; it's about our praise and worship; and it's about evangelism – sharing our faith with others. Yes, '*God loves a cheerful giver.*'

Some time ago, I read the testimony of a chap called Roger Simms, a Christian, who was hitchhiking home, and a Mr Hanover stopped and picked him up. As they drove towards Chicago, Roger felt God urging him to give his testimony and share his faith. He did… and then he asked the man driving if he would like to receive Christ. The long and short of the story is Mr Hanover stopped, bowed his head on the steering wheel and accepted Jesus. Shortly afterwards he dropped Roger at his house and went on to Chicago, which was about an hour down the road.

Years later, while preparing for a business trip to Chicago, Roger came across the business card that Mr Hanover (of Hanover Enterprises) had given him years earlier and he decided to look him up. When he asked the receptionist if he could see Mr Hanover, she said, *'No, but his wife is here.'*

'You knew my husband?' the woman asked. Roger explained that her husband had given him a ride and how he'd led him to Christ.

'When was that?' she asked.

'May 7th, five years ago, the day I was discharged from the army.'

She began to sob. After several minutes she regained

control and said, *'I prayed for my husband for years believing that God would save him. But right after he let you out of his car, on May 7th, he was killed in a head-on collision. I thought God had not answered my prayers.'*

Friends, we need to be generous in sharing our faith with others. Someone may really need to hear it!

3. The third mark of a living, Spirit-filled church is: They are a worshipping church.

'They devoted themselves… to the breaking of bread' (v42). Jesus commanded his followers to remember his death when we gather together in worship. Clearly He didn't want us to forget what happened at Calvary, and Christians have not forgotten. And v46 says: *'Every day they continued to meet together in the temple courts. They broke bread in their homes and ate together with glad and sincere hearts, praising God and enjoying the favour of all the people.'* 'Enjoying the favour of all of the people' – not just believers but people outside of the church as well.

Verse 43 tells us: *'Everyone was filled with awe.'* People saw how these first Christians worshipped and behaved; they saw their generous giving and their love for one another and to those outside the church, and it was a powerful witness. The people – *all of the people* – were filled with awe and with wonder… *'and the Lord added to their number daily those who were being saved'* (v47).

Opportunity doesn't knock on doors it hides behind them. We need to look for opportunities to witness and to evangelise: opportunity knocks of the doors of those who go out seeking it and not (or very rarely) on the doors of those who sit around waiting for it to come to them. Waiting around for someone to ask, *'How do I become a Christian?'* or *'What must I do to be saved?'* is like standing in the middle of a cricket field with your hands cupped together waiting to catch the ball! It just doesn't happen! We must be intentional in looking for opportunities. Evangelist John Chapman used to pray: *'Lord, give me opportunities today – use me to share the gospel with others, and please don't be subtle with me!'* The fact is, so many opportunities are missed because of delay or inertia: as someone has said: *'Too often the opportunity knocks, but by the time you disengage the chain, push back the bolt, unhook the two locks and shut off the burglar alarms, it's too late!'*

4. The fourth mark of a living, Spirit-filled church is: They are a praying church.

'They devoted themselves... to prayer' (v42). Corporate prayer as well as personal prayer: they were a praying church. What do you suppose they prayed for? We are not told specifically, but from the context of the passage they were praying for the spread of the gospel.

There is something uniquely powerful when a church comes together to pray. Prayer meetings create God meetings. Jesus said, *'Where two or three come together in my name, there am I with them.'* (Matthew 18v20)

Stephen Gaukroger writes: 'Praying is like music. Instruments played on their own are good, but there is depth and richness of sound when a number pray together. The Bible promises God's special presence when groups meet for prayer, and it also records some pretty spectacular answers to prayer. Have a look at the story of Peter's miraculous escape from prison, as an example of the power of group prayer (Acts 12v5–17).' [24]

It is been said that the largest room in the world is the room for improvement, so how about if our congregations were to improve and excel in all four marks of church: How about:

- If we grew as a learning church – each of us reading and studying our Bibles more.
- As a generous and sharing church – in giving of our money, time and talents.
- As a worshipping church – in our service and devotion.
- And as a praying church – in our prayers and petitions, especially for the lost.

If our churches really excelled, if each of us were just a little more devoted to the gospel, then do you suppose the Lord might add to our number daily those who are being saved? What do you think?

Group/Church Exercise: One of things I have continually promoted in this book is to be personal. Pushing an invitation through someone's door rarely works. We need to invite people face to face. It is harder, but much more beneficial. The 'scatter gun' approach – inviting anyone and everyone – is not effective in winning disciples for Christ. It is personal evangelism that works best, calling on our relationships to make personal invitations. Now I am not about to contradict what I have said but what follows is an initiative that has increased church attendance at my church significantly, especially at our Easter, Remembrance Day and Christmas Services. (The challenge, of course, is to increase regular weekly attendance but this initiative is building relationships and making in roads.)

One of the things we have done at our church, and which has had a significant impact on mobilising the congregation to become more outward-focused and to get involved in evangelism in the local community, is to introduce a regular prayer drop. (The prayer element is vital otherwise it is not a 'Prayer Drop' but a mail drop!)

The Prayer Drop works like this: we contacted members of the congregation who lived in the parish, asking them if they would deliver literature and pray for their roads at the same time. Once this group was formed, other members of the congregation were asked to 'adopt a road' from those remaining in the parish and for them to do the same. This is important both for the prayer element – that church members should be praying over actual individual homes in the parish – and to focus people to be outward-looking. (The suggested prayer could simply be: 'Lord, may your kingdom come and your will be done in this home.')

The result of this initiative has been significant. In the last year we have seen attendance at our Good Friday and Easter Sunday services increase by 27%, the attendance at our Remembrance Day service increase by 38%, and the attendances at our four main Christmas services increase by a whopping 39% over the previous year's attendance (that is, before we introduced the Prayer Drop).

Practical Tips for Inviting People to an Event: Here are some practical tips for inviting people to a church or to an outreach event (these are taken from the training guide: *Six Steps to Talking About Jesus,* published by Matthias Media):

- Be *intentional*. Plan to invite people to events and always be prepared for unexpected opportunities. Make sure you have invitations/flyers with you. Always be thinking about who you can ask along to events – don't leave everything to the last minute!
- Don't talk yourself out of it. Invite people *confidently*. God is at work! Don't keep talking nervously and start making excuses for them; offer the invitation and then wait for a reply.
- Use *attractive* language to describe the event (as long as it's true), but also let them know it's Christian. If you are

not excited about the event, they won't be!

- Be *realistic*. Expect several knock-backs for every acceptance. For every event, plan to invite three or four people.
- Don't interpret a single knock-back as a sign that you should never invite that person again. It takes *multiple* invitations for some people to say 'Yes'. For others, it may be that that particular event wasn't convenient.
- Link your invitation with a *meal*. If you are inviting people to a morning church meeting, then ask them to come over for lunch afterwards. If you are inviting them to an evening talk, perhaps organize to go out for a coffee. This not only gives you the chance to talk afterwards but also displays your commitment to the friendship.
- Become known as the *'inviter'* by often inviting people to share your life on other occasions (e.g. sport, meals, kids, movies), not just church. People want to know that there is more to the relationship than whether they come along to church with you.
- Organise to *pick them up* or meet them outside the venue. (Then be on time!) No one wants to walk into an unfamiliar environment alone.
- Try asking two or more people to attend *together*. People feel safer in numbers and there is more chance of an acceptance.
- Make sure that you clearly convey the *details* of the event – date, time, location, what the event is about, cost (if any), what to wear, etc. If people are uncertain about anything then they won't say yes, or won't turn up.
- Give them a phone call, email or SMS to *confirm the details* the day before the event. This is particularly worthwhile if your friend is disorganised and might have forgotten.
- Invite people far enough in advance that they have *plenty of notice*, but not so far in advance that they are unlikely to commit themselves.

- Still *attend* even if you have no one to go with. A half-empty room says that what is happening isn't really that important. Also, there will be other guests you can talk with and make feel welcome. (And you can tell your friends what they missed out on!)
- *Pray* constantly for the people you plan to invite.
- Do it because you *love* them and want them to know the love of God displayed in Jesus Christ.[25]

Chapter 6

The Bible and Evangelism

Your word is a lamp to my feet and a light for my path.
— Psalm 119:105

The twelve apostles were evangelists (apostle means sent). Jesus said to his disciples: *'You will receive power when the Holy Spirit comes on you, and you will be my witnesses in Jerusalem, and in all Judea and Samaria, and to the ends of the earth'* (Acts 1:8). And Jesus commissioned his disciples (and us) to go out into all the world and to make more and more disciples: *'Therefore go and make disciples of all nations'* (Matthew 28:19). This is something that has happened — and is continuing to happen today — but from the very outset, the apostles soon found themselves overwhelmed and bogged down with church administrative duties, which could so easily have hampered further evangelism. This is what happened:

After the day of Pentecost the newly Spirit-filled church in Jerusalem began to really take off and grow at a remarkable rate. We are told, for example, in Acts 2:41: *'Those who accepted the message were baptised, and about three thousand were added to their number that day.'* This explosive church growth created its own administrative problems and by the time we get to Acts chapter 6 — and the number of disciples was still increasing (6v1) — a disagreement broke out concerning the unfair distribution of food to those in need. In response the Twelve gathered the church together and told them: *'It would not be right for us to neglect the ministry of the word of God in order to wait on tables'* (6v2). They then chose seven men who were full of the Spirit and wisdom and delegated the administrative responsibility over to them. The reason the disciples did this – and the key text for a growing church perspective – is found in verse 4 where the evangelists said: *'We will give our attention to prayer and ministry of the word.'* In other words, the apostles declared that it's not right to get bogged down with church administration and neglect evangelism and preaching, and so they gave their attention *to prayer and ministry of the word.* (Not exclusively to prayer and Word ministry, but that's where their priority lay, as indeed, should ours, especially if we are reading this book. Too many in our churches get bogged down with maintaining the church at the expense of mission. We need to remember sometimes that Christ came to give us life not meetings!) Bishop Frank Retief, from South Africa, tells his ministers: *'Organise your diary around the fact that, without Christ, people are going to hell.'* [26]

If we are to be effective in evangelism then part of our personal preparation is in studying and meditating on the Scriptures, allowing the word of Christ to dwell in us richly (cf Colossians 3:16), so that we are better equipped and more able to *minister the Word* and communicate God's truth with power and clarity to others. The disciples made the right decision in giving their *attention to prayer and ministry of the word*, and we should do the same. In this section, then, I am going to focus on the Bible *and the ministry of the word of God,* and in the next, we will look at *prayer and evangelism.* My intention is this section, then, is twofold: first, I want to equip you to be able to answer some of the doubts and questions that 'seekers' often pose when it comes to the Bible. And second, I want to encourage you to be spiritually prepared for evangelism by regularly reading the Bible as part of your own personal devotions… so that the Word of God *dwells in you richly.*

> I wonder, how well do you know your Bible? There is a story told about a young lad who brought his friend home from school, but he was embarrassed because his granny was sitting in the armchair reading her Bible. The boy, feeling uncomfortable, turned to his friend and whispered, *'Don't worry about Granny; she's swotting for her finals!'*

When it comes to the Bible people sometimes wonder what the fuss is all about... *'does God really reveal himself to Christians through a book?'*

I used to think like that. I remember when I first picked up a Bible to study and read it earnestly. Years ago, when I first began to explore the Christian faith; I picked up a Bible, determined to read it for myself, and I started to read from page one (which was a mistake). As I recall, I managed to get through about two hundred pages, reading through Genesis, Exodus and Leviticus before I finally gave up, threw in the towel and came to the conclusion that the Bible was a dead book full of dry, lifeless words, and at the time, it puzzled me that anyone else could think otherwise. (The problem was I started in the wrong place! The Old Testament sets out the problem but it stops short of giving us the answer to the problem; that doesn't come until the New Testament. I should have started there.) Later on, however, after I became a Christian and the Holy Spirit entered my life, I picked up the Bible again and this time the words came alive and God spoke to me on every page, and I gained insights and inspiration that I had just not seen on my first reading. Of course, what made the difference was that now I knew the Author! When you know the author of a book or a letter the reading of it takes on a whole new dimension. Now I love the Word of God and I read my Bible daily, and have done for many years. Indeed, the Bible is like a love letter to us from God and it has become one of my most treasured possessions.

Let me share a piece of sentimentality, written by an unknown author and which was given to me on a card with the heading:

'A Note From A Friend'. It reads a bit like a love letter – a little soppy, perhaps – but I'd like you to see through that and try to focus on the underlying message:

> My Dear Friend
> How are you? I just had to send a note to tell you how much I care about you. I saw you yesterday as you were talking to your friends; I waited all day hoping you would want to talk with me too. I gave you a beautiful sunset to close your day and a warm breeze to comfort you, and I waited, but you never came. It saddened me... but I still love you and I am still your friend.
>
> I saw you sleeping last night and longed to be with you so I spilled moonlight on your face and, again I waited, wanting to rush down so we could talk. I have so many gifts for you! You woke up and rushed off to work. My heart was heavy again.
>
> If you would only listen to me! I love you! I try to tell you in the blue skies, and in the green grass. I whisper it in the leaves on the trees, I breathe it in the colours of flowers; I shout it to you in the mountain streams and give the birds love songs to sing. My love for you is deeper than the ocean and bigger than the biggest need in your heart! Ask me! Talk with me! Please don't ignore me or forget about me. I have so much to share with you! I won't trouble you any further. I won't force myself upon you. It is your decision. I have chosen you and I'll wait... for a while longer yet, because I love you. (Signed) Jesus.

The Bible is like a love letter to us from God and as Paul Little, the professor of evangelism at Trinity Evangelical Divinity School, once noted: *'The people that God used to record His words in the Bible were themselves uncommonly moved by them.'* They said the Word of God is: *'honey in my mouth'* (Ezekiel 3:3); *'spiritual food for the hungry'* (Job 23:12); *'dwelling in me richly'* (Colossians 3:16); *'a lamp for my feet'* (Psalm 119:105); *'a joy and delight to my heart'* (Jeremiah 15:16); *'renewing my mind'* (Romans 12:2); *'a fire that burns in my heart'* (Jeremiah 20:9); *'more precious than gold'* (Psalm 19:10); *'sharper than a two-edged sword'* (Hebrews 4:12); *'a great reward'* (Psalm 19:11); *'true and righteous'* (Psalm 119:160); *'penetrating my thoughts and attitudes'* (Hebrews 4:12); *'perfect and trustworthy'* (Psalm 19:7).[27]

If we are to be effective in our evangelism and making disciples (not just making converts) we, like the apostles, need also to give our attention to the ministry of the word – to preaching the gospel, and teaching and training other disciples. Young and old Christians need to be involved in a church that is faithful to Scripture and alive in the Spirit, and that meets regularly for Bible study, fellowship and prayer so that we grow together in Christ. Here's a good illustration you can use, maybe on a Christian nurture course or when chatting to people who are exploring Christianity:

> **An illustration using a candle or tea light and a glass jar:** Light the candle and place it in on a saucer. Ask, the question: will the candle go out if I place a glass jar on top of it, yes or no? Place the jar on top of the candle and the flame will go out after a few seconds as the oxygen in the jar is depleted. Application: In order for our light to continue to shine we need to feed our faith through Bible study, prayer, fellowship and church.

Hebrews 4:12 tells us: *'the word of God is living and active. Sharper than any double-edged sword, it penetrates even to dividing soul and spirit, joints and marrow; it judges the thoughts and attitudes of the heart.'* The Word of God speaks to us. *'But how does it speak to us'*, people may ask; *'how is the word of God living and active?'* To answer that I want to look at three related issues or topics that I have often taught on *Alpha, Christianity Explored* and *Just Looking* courses, namely: how God has revealed Himself to us through the Bible; how God speaks to us through the Bible; and, how God feeds and nurtures us through the Bible.

How God has revealed Himself to us through the Bible

God wrote the Bible. He used human agents to write down the actual words but God is the author. The apostle Peter penned these words: *'[the Bible] never had its origins in the will of man, but men spoke from God as they were carried along by the Holy Spirit'* (2 Peter 1:21). God has revealed Himself to us through the Scriptures. 2 Timothy 3:16 states: *'All Scripture is God-breathed and is useful for teaching, rebuking, correcting and training in righteousness.'* In other words, God inspired the writing of the Scriptures to tell us what is right (*teaching*), what is not right (*rebuking*), how to get it right (*correcting*), and how to live staying right (*training in righteousness*).

When Paul wrote the second letter to Timothy and said, *'All Scripture is God-breathed...'* most of the New Testament hadn't actually been written by then, but we should note that the apostle Peter held that Paul's writings were also Scripture (Paul wrote 13 of the 27 books in the New Testament), and Peter said: *'Our dear brother Paul also wrote to you with the wisdom that God gave him. (...) His letters contain some things that are hard to understand, which ignorant and unstable people distort, as they do the other Scriptures, to their own destruction'* (2 Peter 3:15–16).

People often ask: *'How do we know that what the Bible says is right; how do we know it is actually true – just because it says it's true are we to take it at face value?'* Well, there is lots of evidence to corroborate what the Bible says is factual and accurate (we will look this shortly) but at the end of the day, accepting the Word of God as being right and true has always been, and will always be, a question of faith. It's a bit like asking the question, how do you know your spouse loves you? We accept it by faith but we can generally tell when someone loves us, not just because they say they do, but also because they demonstrate their love in many and various ways. It is the same with God.

Is there any proof, then, that the Bible, the inspired Word of God, is true?

The answer to that question is yes. Apart from the personal testimony – witness statements, if you like – of countless millions of Christians down through the ages, there is plenty of other hard evidence that the Bible is indeed trustworthy. Let me give you a few facts and some examples to show you what I mean.

The Bible is a holy book – we call it the *Holy Bible* – but there is nothing holy, religious or spiritual about the word 'bible', which is derived from the Latin word 'biblia,' and simply means books. The Bible is actually a collection of 66 books (39 in the Old Testament and 27 in the New) written by at least 40 different authors, who had various professions such as kings, scholars, historians, prophets, poets, fishermen, a doctor and of course, apostles of Christ. The genre of literature is also varied and includes history, story-narrative, poetry, wisdom writings, prophecy, biographies (gospels), letters and apocalyptic literature.

The earliest books are from around Moses' time (15th century BC) and the latest from the end of the 1st century, around 95AD, so the material was published, collected and brought together over a period of around 1500 years. Although the books are not in chronological order there is a clear and definite logic to the way they have been assembled, an amazing development of common themes and an overall unity. It truly is an outstanding piece of literature. *'Out of this world,'* some would say!

Others might not agree. Sometimes people object and say: *'Surely you can't (or don't have to) believe everything you read in the Bible.'* The first thing I want to say in response is that we do not need to believe or agree with everything that is written in the Bible before making a decision for Christ. Secondly, and let's be clear here, Christians do not venerate or worship a book. We are not called to believe in a book, as such, we are called to believe in Jesus Christ as revealed to us in and through this holy book. The main point of the Bible is to show us how to enter into and remain in a relationship with God through Jesus.

It's a bit like when someone brings a new baby into church. We don't admire the buggy and say, *'Oh what a lovely upholstered buggy: truly an outstanding design and manufactured with such skill.'* We don't admire the buggy we admire the baby contained within the buggy. Similarly with the Bible, Christians don't revere or worship a book, but God who is revealed to us in and through the book.

The Bible we have today is known as the complete or closed 'canon' of Scripture, that is, those books that are recognised as being the inspired Word of God. The New Testament canon first became established in 367A.D., when Athanasius − known as the father of orthodoxy − listed all of the books of the New Testament in his thirty-ninth Paschal Letter, and the canon was also later confirmed at a gathered church council in Carthage in 397A.D. The word 'canon' comes from the rule of law that was used to determine if a book measured up to a particular standard. Three criteria were used in recognising and acknowledging canonicity; these were:

1. was the book known to be apostolic in its origin − that is, did the book derive from the teaching of the apostles?
2. was the attitude towards such a book as inspired Scripture, accepted and recognized by the early churches?
3. did the book promote sound doctrine and truth?[28]

Here are some more facts: The Bible is the world's all time out and out bestseller: it has far outsold any other book in history and remains on the best sellers list year after year. Currently there are 44 million copies of the Bible sold each year, and that figure continues to grow annually. Nothing comes anywhere near it. To date the Bible, or parts of it, have been translated into over 1,240 languages worldwide, and there are translation projects currently under way for more than 450 further languages.[29]

Time and again critics will say (usually because they have heard it somewhere else first), *'the Bible contradicts itself and is full of errors'*, but I have personally read the Bible through several times and I've never found any. It's true that there are a number of (minor) differences in the way some of the authors report certain events − the Bible says *'all Scripture is God-breathed'* [God-inspired]; it does not say it is God dictated − but the Bible never contradicts itself.

One typical example of a 'supposed' contradiction surrounds Jesus' second coming: The Bible teaches that Jesus will one day return to earth. In Matthew's Gospel (24:40–41) we read that at the precise moment Jesus returns: *'Two men will be in a field (...) and two women will be grinding with a hand mill,'* – which would seem to indicate that Jesus' return will be during daylight hours, when people are at work. However Luke's Gospel (17:42) says: *'on that night two people will be in one bed'* (night time?): This looks like a glaring error or contradiction, until we remember that the middle of the day in one part of the world is the middle of the night in another. The Bible does not contradict itself.

It is fair to say that many people have tried to disprove the Bible, or they have searched for flaws to try and discredit it, and in doing so many have also ended up being converted. Such is the power of God's Word: it has stood the test of time. Sir Isaac Newton was an avid student of Scripture, after years of diligent study he came to the conclusion that the Bible was *'a rock from which all hammers of criticism have never chipped a single fragment.'*[30] One poet describes the Bible as 'The Anvil of God's Word' and wrote this:

Last eve I passed beside a blacksmith's door,
and heard the anvil ring the vesper chime;
then, looking in, I saw upon the floor
old hammers, worn with beating years of time.
'How many anvils have you had,' said I,
'to wear and batter all these hammers so?'
'Just one,' said he, and then with twinkling eye,
'The anvil wears the hammers out, you know.'
And so, thought I, the anvil of God's Word,
For ages sceptic blows have beat upon;
Yet, though the noise of falling blows was heard,
The anvil is unharmed – the hammers gone. (Anon)

Sometimes people say: *'How do we know the words of the Bible haven't been lost in translation; how do we know the Bible is accurate?'* The answer to that is simple: the accuracy of what has been written, copied, and passed down through the centuries is remarkable. The Bible is indeed a precise translation of the original texts. We know this because we can compare it to the original manuscripts. There are some 24,300 ancient manuscripts or fragments of scripture known to be in existence today. The oldest fragments of New Testament Scripture are a piece of papyrus containing part of John's gospel dating back to between 117–138AD (which is exhibited in John Ryeland's Library in Manchester), and three fragments of papyrus in Magdalen College, Oxford that have been dated to the third quarter of the first century (i.e. somewhere between 42–66 years after Christ's death). Also in 1947 the Dead Sea Scrolls were discovered. These contained fragments of every book in the Old Testament (except Esther), and included the complete book of Isaiah. The scrolls have been dated to around 100BC and the discovery of them has proved beyond any shadow of doubt that the Bible we have today is an authentic copy and translation of the original documents. So, the Bible is accurate, very accurate.

We should also remember that Jesus quoted scripture often. The only 'Bible' Jesus had at that time was the Old Testament, but Jesus is recorded as quoting verbatim from it nearly forty times (from thirteen different books), and he also referred to Scripture on many other occasions.[31] But more than any of this, Jesus himself is the most compelling proof that the Bible is God inspired and true. Jesus fulfilled Scripture and, indeed, He will fulfil what few prophecies remain in the Scriptures when He returns. On the subject of the Bible being God inspired, or God-breathed, John Benton, author of *Looking for the Answer,* makes the valid point that the Bible's prophetic teaching is *'probably the most direct evidence for the special involvement of God with this book'.*[32] Let me share a visual aid to help illustrate the point:

David Watson told of one biblical scholar who worked out that there are 332 distinct prophecies in the Old Testament, which were literally fulfilled in the person of Jesus. He further worked out that the mathematical probability of all these prophecies being fulfilled in just one man is 1 in 84, followed by 97 zeros. That figure looks like this: [33]

1 in 84
000
00000
000000000
00000000000
000000000000000
0000000000000
00000000000
000000000
00000
000

Now just how accurate that figure is, or how someone actually goes about calculating such mathematical probabilities – or even how to pronounce how many zillion, trillion, billion, million that figure represents – is beyond me, but I wanted to show this illustration to, at least, provide some perspective on how improbably it really is that Jesus isn't the promised Saviour or Messiah that the Old Testament prophets spoke about.

The Bible is God's word, God's revelation to mankind. As I said earlier, if we are to be effective in our evangelism and making disciples we need to *give our attention to the ministry of the word* – to preaching the gospel, and teaching and training other disciples from the word of God. In Matthew's Gospel (4:4) Jesus said, *'Man does not live on bread alone, but on every word that comes from the mouth of God.'* That means we must rely on God's word for our spiritual food, and we must teach and train and encourage others to do likewise. Also, as I said earlier, we need to be spiritually prepared for evangelism by regularly reading the Bible as part of our own personal devotions… so that the Word of God *dwells in us richly.* So let's now look at…

How God speaks to us through the Bible

I remember shortly after I became a Christian, asking an older Christian for some advice because I was concerned about spiritual dryness: I didn't want to ever lose my newfound faith, or for my relationship with Christ to ever grow cold or stale (which seemed to have happened with older members of the church)! My friend at the time gave me one of the best pieces of advice a mature Christian can give to a new believer, or to any believer for that matter: He told me, *'Ian, every day read your Bible and pray.'* He compared our relationship to God to be like a marriage, saying that the more we communicate, share and spend time with our spouse the deeper and more meaningful our relationship and love for each other. And it's the same with our relationship with God: the more time we spend in his presence, in prayer and in his Word, the stronger and deeper our relationship and faith will be. I'm glad to say that I took my friends advice, and doing so has had a major impact on my life.

The Bible is such a powerful a book it literally changes people's lives – if they allow it to, that is! We read earlier from Hebrews 4v12:*'the word of God is living and active'* – but how is it living and active? Well, unlike any other book in the whole world, every time we pick up the Bible and read it the author is present! God speaks to us through his Word. The famous nineteenth century preacher, Charles Spurgeon wrote, *'We are blessed to have God's Word always to guide us. Without a compass the mariner would be lost. So would Christians without the Bible. This is the unerring chart in which is described all the channels from the quick sands of destruction to the haven of salvation by one who knows all the way.'*[34] And what happens when God speaks through the preaching or reading of his Word? Nicky Gumbel reminds us that God brings the gift of faith to those who are not yet Christians.[35] In the book of Romans (10:17), Paul says: *'Faith comes from hearing the message, and the message is heard through the word of Christ.'* And in John's Gospel, the evangelist tells us that he has only written about a select few of Jesus' miracles but John says, *'These are written that you may believe that Jesus is the Christ, the Son of God, and that by believing you may have life in his name'* (John 20:31). It is often as people read about Jesus in the Bible that they come to faith in Him. I have seen this happen time and time again on our own 'explorers courses' where we often use Mark's Gospel as a starting point to explore Jesus' story – who He is, what He taught, and how that relates to our story. For many of the seekers who join the course, Jesus walks off the pages of Mark's gospel and into their hearts.

God speaks to us through His word, to guide us, and direct us, and change us to become more like Jesus. The famous evangelist D.L. Moody said: *'The Bible was not given to increase our knowledge, but to change our lives.'* There are lots of good reasons why we should read the Bible: Spending time in God's presence and listening to his Word often brings joy and peace in times of crisis, or hope in the times of despair. The Bible is like a guidebook – it tells us how we should live our lives; it provides direction when we are lost or not sure which path to take; and it answers many of life's questions. Reading the Bible also feeds us and encourages us and warns us. God's word acts like a spiritual antibiotic, providing protection against the world, the flesh and the devil; it also provides defence against spiritual attack – remember Jesus quoted Scripture to satan when he was tempted in the desert. Reading the Bible has the power to change us, making us more and more like Christ. As someone wisely put it: The BIBLE stands for *'Best Instruction Before Life Ends'*.

Often critics of the Bible say that it is full of rules – 'Thou shalt not do this or that' – which seek to confine and restrict our lives, but Jesus didn't come to constrain us, He came to set us free. Jesus said, *'I have come that they may have life, and have it to the full'* (John 10:10). On that note, I wonder if we Christians have sometimes forgotten what the whole of the gospel is! It seems that many in our churches – not all but many – have inadvertently reduced the gospel message to the forgiveness of sins and life after death. It seems that the *'good news'* has been limited to *'repent and believe to receive forgiveness of your sins now and eternal life later'* – which, from my experience, people do not always perceive as either being *good* or *news*, because it doesn't seem to impact on life now or have anything compelling to say about life before we die. But when Jesus said: *'I have come that they may have life, and have it to the full,'* He was talking about us having life to the full in Him now, not when we die. The gospel is good news for now… and it will be absolutely fantastic news later on!

Let me illustrate with a story: There were two frogs at the bottom of a well. One frog looked up at the sky and thought that the world was only as big as the top of the well. This frog lived out the rest of his life at the bottom of the well, in his own self-imposed confines. (His gospel was limited.) The other frog looked up and figured there is more to life than meets the eye, so he climbed the wall and when he reached the top he saw just how much more there actually is.

When Jesus said: *'I have come that they may have life to the full,'* He was talking about us being able to have life to the full in Him now, not when we die.

The gospel is not all 'pie in the sky when you die'; it's also 'meat on the plate while you wait!' Rick Richardson, director of evangelism at Wheaton College in America, says: *'When Jesus announced the good news of the kingdom, which is the in-breaking and dynamic rule of God to set all things right, he wasn't talking about what would happen after people died. He was talking about the personal and social transformation that had begun with his coming. The news was good because God was setting all things right.'*[36] The gospel is not just a promissory note; it's not all future benefits. Christians are also meant to enjoy wonderful and abundant life now, and this includes blessings such as freedom and release from the burdens of guilt; forgiveness of sins; the gift of faith; being endowed with amazing spiritual gifts to enable us to serve the church (see Romans 12:6–8, 1 Corinthians 12, Ephesians 4:11–12); healings and miraculous answers to prayer; our discovering true meaning and purpose in life; having the Holy Spirit dwell within us; knowing God personally and experiencing the peace of Christ; having joy and hope; knowing that we are accepted and belong; enjoying the fellowship, love and support of the family of believers, and so on and so forth. No, the good news it is not all pie in the sky when you die; Christians are meant to enjoy abundant life now… even if the best is yet to come!

Coming back to my earlier point that critics of the Bible are often claiming the Scriptures seek to confine and restrict us: Jesus did not come to constrain us but to set us free so that we *'may have life, and have it to the full'*. The Bible is like a guidebook that provides us with boundaries so that we can live as God intended us to live. These boundaries are not there to restrict us, in the sense of oppressing us, but to protect us from ourselves and from others dangers.

A while ago I heard about a nursery school situated on the corner of a busy road, with traffic constantly driving past. The school had a lovely playground, surrounded by small metal railings to stop the children running into the road. However, at break times all the children would stay very close to the school building because they were frightened of the passing traffic on the other side of the low railings. Then one day the school brought in builders to erect a higher steel-mesh fence and from that day on, the children played in the whole of the playground. Why did this make such a difference? Well, because the children were a lot happier and felt much more secure when the fences were put up to show clear boundaries. It is the same with us: If we stay within the boundaries that God has set for us and we live by His rules, then there is freedom and joy. But if we cheat or break the rules people get hurt!

The Bible gives us clear boundaries for our well-being, happiness and safety. When the Word of God says, *'Do not commit adultery'* or *'do not covet your neighbour's wife'*, it's not because God wants to restrict and oppress us or be a killjoy, but because He knows the pain and misery and suffering, and the lasting damage to relationships that such sins cause. God loves us and He wants to protect us: He wants us to be safe and happy and to enjoy life the way He intended us to do. Millions of products around the world carry this piece of advice: *'For the best results follow the maker's instructions'*. That same message is stamped indelibly on every human heart! That's why God gave us the Bible, so we could follow our Maker's instructions.

How God feeds and nurtures us through the Bible

The Bible is one of the main sources of nourishment for a Christian. It's great to hear the Bible preached and taught when we come to church on a Sunday or in a midweek group, but we need to have our *'daily bread'* if we are to remain fit and strong and healthy. And also to be effective in evangelism, as I said earlier, part of our preparation is in studying and meditating on the Scriptures, allowing the word of Christ to dwell in us richly (Colossians 3:16), so we are better equipped and more able to communicate God's truth with authority to others. There is no substitute for a daily quiet time alone with God, gathering fresh sustenance from his Word. The only way you or I can ever really get to know one other, not just know about each other, is for us to spend time together. Similarly, with God: if we – and those we disciple – want to know God more, if we want to love him and know his love for us more, then we really need to read our Bible, regularly and diligently. Not just to read it going through the motions, like a tick box exercise, because then the words just flow through our mind like water gushing through a pipe – nothing sticks! We need to read it thoughtfully, prayerfully, expectantly and daily.

How then do we hear God speak to us through the Bible; how does he feed and nurture us? Let me share a personal example to illustrate: A few days after I first wrote this section, a close Christian friend of mine called Gerry Muldowney – who was like a spiritual father to me – died suddenly of a heart attack. The day after I discovered the news I couldn't sleep and in the early hours I came downstairs to pray and to read my Bible. God spoke to me very clearly, words of comfort and truth. The Holy Spirit reminded me of a number of specific verses, which came to my mind one after another – I wrote them in my journal: '*Then I heard a voice from heaven say, 'Blessed are the dead who die in the Lord from now on'* (Revelation 14v13); '*No eye has seen, no ear has heard, no mind has conceived what God has prepared for those who love him*' (1 Corinthians 2v9); '*Well done, good and faithful servant...Come and share your master's happiness*' (Matthew 25v21); '*Do not let your hearts be troubled. Trust in God; trust also in me. In my Father's house are many rooms; if it were not so, I would have told you. And if I go and prepare a place for you, I will come back and take you to be with me where I am*' (John 14v1–3). God led me to these verses so that I would be comforted in my grief and assured of His sovereignty. God speaks to us and feeds and nurtures us through the Bible, which is why I always try to encourage others to read it regularly and diligently. Besides which, the Scriptures you don't read can't help you.

Someone said to me recently, '*Ian, You don't have to read the Bible or go to church to be a Christian.*' And I responded, '*No you don't, that's true! And likewise you don't have to talk to your spouse or go home for you to be married, but then what kind of marriage would that be?*' The fact is we can't grow in our relationship with God if we don't really spend any time with Him in prayer and in the Scriptures. Now, maybe you find reading the Bible difficult, many I know don't, and that's great, but for others, what can you do? There's a saying that '*if you fail to plan you plan to fail*'. If we're going to spend regular time reading and feeding on God's word, and being spiritually prepared for personal evangelism, then we really need to plan ahead, otherwise we'll never do it, simply because other pressures on our time will crowd out our Bible reading. Don't quit with the programme or feel bad if you don't manage to keep to your plan 100% of the time, just start over again. Falling behind is sometimes inevitable and we all have a day off or oversleep occasionally! But seven days without reading the Bible makes one weak (spiritually)!

In closing, may God open your eyes to see wonderful things in His word as you read and study the Bible, and may the words of Christ *dwell in you richly* as you preach and teach and reach out to others with the gospel.

Practical Tips for regular Bible reading: The truth is you can't watch television for three hours then read your Bible or a Christian devotional for three minutes and expect God to bless you with spiritual growth!' As Galatians 6v7 says *'A man reaps what he sows.'*

- Form the habit of spending time each day reading the Bible, maybe just a chapter a day. But don't rush. The aim isn't to see how quickly we can through it but to see what we can get out of it! It's the quality of time that matters not the quantity. It's much better to reflect and mull over a single verse than to speed read and not absorb anything.
- Chose a time that works for you. Many people (myself included) find that first thing in the morning is the best time, but maybe a mid-morning or an afternoon break or last thing at night suits you better. Whatever time works best for you stick with it, and guard this time jealously.
- Use daily Bible reading notes or commentaries as an aid to help you understand the Word of God. There are lots of good ones available; try one or two and see how you get on. (I have used *Explore* [37] Bible reading notes daily for several years.)
- Find a place where can go and not be disturbed, and pray before you start, asking God to help you understand what you read, and to show you how to apply what you learn. I often use Psalm 119v18 as a prayer: *'open my eyes that I may see wonderful things in your law.'* If you come to the Bible hungry and expectant to learn, your Bible reading will become a place of nurture and growth, as

well as a source of guidance, strength and encouragement each day.

- As you read look for God on every page, then look for yourself on the same page: Ask how is this applicable to me today? What is God saying to me? Is there something in this passage that I should pray about?
- For new Christians or those just starting out in reading the Bible, I always recommend a great place to start is Luke's gospel (24 chapters, so read one a day over three and a bit weeks) then read the book of Acts (see how the early church started, grew and spread), then maybe read Philippians and the Psalms.

Chapter 7

Prayer and Evangelism

'We will give our attention to prayer and ministry of the word.'
– Acts 6:4

Charles Spurgeon once said, *'A neglect of prayer is the beginning of all spiritual decline.'* (Think about that for a moment.) Conversely, the people who are most on fire for the Lord are the believers who pray and commune with God... a lot! When the great eighteenth-century evangelist John Wesley was asked, *'Why do people seem to be drawn to you, almost like a magnet?'* he replied, *'When you set yourself on fire for the gospel, people love to come and see you burn!'* If we are to be effective in evangelism then our spiritual preparation must begin, continue and end with prayer.

Jesus said if we remain connected to the vine we will bear much fruit (John 15:5). If we want to know God more intimately and grow in our relationship with Him; if we want to be more open to the Spirit and hear His voice speaking to us; if we want to *set ourselves on fire for the gospel* and be more effective in evangelism and reaching out to the lost, then we need to *remain connected to the vine* and spend time in our heavenly Father's presence, quality time. Have you ever noticed how some Christians can turn up to a worship service, a prayer meeting or a Bible study group and they seem to be able to immediately connect and engage with the Holy Spirit and enjoy quality time and intimacy in worship, prayer or fellowship? Mostly, the reason this happens is because the believer has invested quantity time with the Lord first. The fact is, in any relationship, whether it's with God or spending time with family or loved ones, usually you can only enjoy quality time if you have put in quantity time first! Many hard working busy people say it's the quality of time that counts and not so much the quantity of time. But that saying is a load of old baloney, probably made up by some overworked executive to ease his guilty conscience. The fact is you can only enjoy quality time if you put in quantity time!

Psalm 139v1–4 says: *'O LORD, you have searched me and you know me. You know when I sit and when I rise; you perceive my thoughts from afar. You discern my going out and my lying down; you are familiar with all my ways. Before a word is on my tongue you know it completely, O LORD.'* These verses teach us that God knows our thoughts and what we are going to say even before we say it. Our thoughts are like words to God (which is why we don't need to pray out loud to be heard). And Jesus told us: *'Your Father knows what you need before you ask him'* (Matthew 6:8). Why then do we need to ask? What is the point of prayer? Well, what kind of a relationship would it be if there was no communication? Calvin summarised our need to pray like this:

> *'Believers do not pray with the view of informing God about things unknown to him, or of exciting him to do his duty, or of urging him as though he were reluctant. On the contrary, they pray in order that they may arouse themselves to seek him, that they may exercise their faith in meditating on his promises, that they may relieve themselves from their anxieties by pouring them into his bosom; in a word that they may declare that from him alone they hope and expect, both for themselves and for others, all good things.'*

It is through prayer that we get to know God. God wants us to pray and He loves it when we pray because prayer is relational. We are not just ventilating vertically, we are dialoguing with God, praying (out loud or silently) and listening. Soren Kierkegaard once observed: *'A man prayed, and at first he thought prayer was talking. But he became more and more quiet until in the end he realised that prayer is [also] listening.'* Immediately we begin to pray we move into the spiritual realm and God's presence is a reality with us, whether we are physically aware of it or not. Our praying acknowledges our dependence on God to guide, protect and provide for us. Our praying initiates communication, fellowship and relationship. And our praying is also glorifying to God because it shows that we are seeking him and wanting to be in relationship and communion with him. Bishop J.C. Ryle once voiced it like this: [God says,] *'Abide in me. Cling to me. Stick fast to me. Live the life of close and intimate communion with me. Get nearer and nearer to me. Roll every burden on me. Cast your whole weight on me. Never let go of your hold on me for a moment.'*

God desires to have an intimate relationship with us. He searches for those who seek Him and He promises... *'Those who seek me find me'* (Proverbs 8:17). Just as our relationships with each other are deepened and strengthened when we regularly communicate and spend time together, so our relationship with God when we read our Bible, meditate and pray. This is something we may need to prioritise in our daily routine. That's what Jesus did: Jesus often went off by himself to a solitary place in order to pray (cf Mark 1:35, Luke 5:12.) It may mean that we have to delegate other stuff to free up the time to do this. That's what the disciples did. They made a deliberate choice and said: *'It would not be right for us to neglect the ministry of the word of God in order to wait on tables... We will give our attention to prayer and ministry of the word'* (Acts 6:2, 4). The disciples didn't allow themselves to get so bogged down with 'other stuff' that they neglected preaching and evangelism, and they deliberately gave their attention *to prayer and ministry of the word.*

In fact, all the early believers took prayer seriously and the New Testament church was actually conceived in prayer. You may recall that just before Jesus ascended to heaven (forty days after His resurrection) He told the apostles not to leave Jerusalem until they had received the gift of Holy Spirit (cf. Acts 1:3–4). Ten days later, at Pentecost, the outpouring of Holy Spirit happened. But in that ten-day interim period (between Ascension and

Pentecost) what do you suppose the gathered believers were doing while they waited around in Jerusalem? Acts 1v14 gives us the answer: *'They all joined together constantly in prayer.'* Indeed, the New Testament church was conceived in prayer. And when the outpouring happened at Pentecost, and everyone present was filled with the Holy Spirit (Acts 2:4), what happened next? They launched a church that it is still impacting the world today, some two thousand years later. Think about it, every other Christian fellowship in the world today is, in one way or another, a church plant connected to the first New Testament church in Jerusalem and conceived by the prayers of the early believers who, we are told, were devoted to prayer (cf Acts 2:42).

> Talking of prayer, there's a story told about a family who invited the minister over for dinner, and when he arrived and sat down at the table the mother asked her five-year-old to say grace. Puzzled, the child asked, *'What should I say?'* Her mum replied, *'Just say what you've heard me say, dear.'* So, bowing her head reverently, the little girl prayed, *'Dear God, why on earth did I invite the minister over for dinner?'*

More seriously, John Bunyan once said: *'You can do more than pray after you have prayed but you can't do more than pray until you've prayed.'* This is a very practical book. It is full of no-nonsense advice, ideas, suggestions and things we can do to empower and mobilise the local church to get more involved in outreach and evangelism, but first and foremost, and before we attempt to do any of these things, we too need to pray. Prayer is to ministry like a beating heart is to a living body. Prayer is at the heart of the Christian faith because it's about our relationship with God and, as such, prayer is also the most important activity of our lives. Prayer should be central to everything we do – before, during and after we do it. In a word, prayer is essential because God has ordained that our prayers play an important part in his providential answers. To put it another way, the reason that God answers prayer is because his children ask him to. As one poet wrote: *'Games can't be won unless they are played, and prayers can't be answered unless they are prayed.'*

Jesus told his disciples that they should always pray and not give up (Luke 18:1). And Paul reiterated Jesus' teaching, in 1 Thessalonians 5:17, when he said that we are to *'pray continually'* (NIV) or *'pray without ceasing'* (KJV). Our persistence in prayer is not so that we might pester God, as it were, so that He submits to our will, but to demonstrate that we are serious about what we pray for, and to keep active and open the lines of communication so that we will know how and when God is prompting us to act or serve. Prayer should be at the centre of everything we do. The call is to pray continually, without ceasing, and with all kinds of prayers (Ephesians 6:18). But let's be honest, we do struggle here sometimes, don't we? I mean prayer is difficult at times, isn't it? When we're tired, run down, overworked with so many other important things to do, making time for prayer is sometimes… well, a bit of a luxury, isn't it? But shouldn't we rather make it a daily discipline; shouldn't we make it a prior priority to pray? It's true that sometimes we may not feel like praying but I often find the hardest part of prayer is usually just getting started!

Many people, like myself, find a daily quiet time is the best way to remain focused and in communion with the Lord throughout the day. For the last twenty years (ever since I became a Christian) I have had a daily quiet time first thing in the morning, where I read my Bible, pray and wait on the Lord. My own discipline is this: 'No Bible No Breakfast'. I want to pray and feed spiritually on the word of God before I seek to feed myself physically. (Find what works for you.) There is absolutely no substitute for a daily quiet time alone with God. Many people jump out of bed in the morning and dash off into the day without giving God so much as a second thought; others prioritise their day and begin in prayer. Some wake up and say, *'Good lord it's morning!'* others wake up and say, *'Good morning, Lord.'* Guess which group enjoys a more intimate relationship with God. And guess which group are more effective in evangelism. John Bunyan also said this: *'He who runs from God in the morning will scarcely find Him in the rest of the day.'*

Practical Tip: Always be praying for non-believers around you. Someone once faithfully prayed for you: Who was it? (My grandmother faithfully prayed for me for years. She died in 1992. I became a Christian the following year! Don't ever give up praying. Even when we think our prayers go unanswered, God hears them.) We should always be praying for those closest to us who are not yet following Christ; asking that God would open their eyes spiritually to see who Jesus is. We should pray for those who God has laid on our hearts; that they would come to know and accept Jesus for themselves. Create a pray list or a prayer diary for people who are on your heart and pray fervently for them. Pray with your heart as well as your lips.

On the subject of prayer Ronald Dunn writes: '*Satan has no defence against this weapon; he does not have an anti-prayer missile. For instance, the unbeliever has many defences against our evangelistic efforts. He can refuse to attend church, and if he does occasionally show up, he can shift into neutral and count the cracks in the ceiling. You can go to his home, but he doesn't have to let you in. Hand him a tract on the street, and he can throw it away. Get on TV, and he can switch channels. Call him on the phone, and he can hang up. But he cannot prevent the Lord Jesus from knocking on the door of his heart in response to our intercession. People we cannot reach any other way can be reached by way of the throne of grace.*'[38]

St Sebastian's Church in Wokingham (St Sebs), where I am currently serving as a minister, has a very healthy number of men who are committed members of the church – more so than many other churches I know. However, as with most churches today, there are also a number of women members whose husbands or partners don't come to church. When I began my ministry at St Sebs I asked the church administrator for a list of husbands who didn't attend church, but whose wives were committed members of the congregation, and I was given a list with the names of twenty-nine men on it. A number of us in the church then began to pray for these men. Today as I write this, some twenty months later, six of these husbands are now regularly attending the church and three of them to my knowledge have now made a personal commitment to Christ.

It's not a revival yet, for sure, and I wish the numbers were higher – God give us more! But in answer to our prayers there are at least six Christian women whose husbands now sit beside them on Sunday mornings, and the level of faith and expectation within the church is increasing. One of these six Christian women has been praying for her husband for twenty years!

Christian wives should continue to pray for their unbelieving husbands (and Christian husbands for their unbelieving wives). In 1 Peter 3:1–2 we are told: *'Wives, in the same way be submissive to your husbands'* – that doesn't mean be a doormat, it means be like Christ. Why? Peter continues, *'So that, if any of them do not believe the word, they may be won over without words by the behaviour of their wives'* – and visa versa – *'when they see the purity and reverence of your lives.'* There is something profoundly attractive and deeply compelling when people see the purity and reverence of a godly life. Christian educator and writer Henry Blackaby gave this counsel and testimony: *'I have known many a Christian who was deeply concerned because a husband or wife is an unbeliever. As the result, the believer would continually speak to his or her partner about the need for God. However, this persistence at times actually frustrated the non-believer and drove the spouse further from God. When the Christians come to me and tearfully share that they have done all they know to do but their mate seems more reluctant than ever, I suggest they may be attempting to do what only the Holy Spirit can do. "Instead of* trying to convict your spouse of sin," I say, "pray for your spouse daily and then watch to see when the Holy Spirit prepares him or her for a spiritual conversation.'" [39] That's good advice and, of course, it also applies to children and to other family members too.

The Bible teaches that no 'sinner' ever seeks after God… at least not by themselves! (Romans 3:11) Therefore God must seek the 'sinner' (cf. Genesis 3:8–10, Luke 19:19). Jesus himself said, *'No one can come to me unless the Father who sent me draws them to me'* (John 6:44 NLT). We need to pray that God would open blind eyes and draw people, including our loves ones who are lost, to Jesus. Pray for God's mercy. Pray that their names may be written in His book of life. Pray for an awakening, and keep on keeping on.

The Bible teaches that God wants all men to be saved (1 Timothy 2:4); God wants everyone to come to repentance (2 Peter 3:9), but He will not force salvation on anyone. It is a free invitation open to all, but it's an invitation that must accepted to become validated. We need to pray that God would draw people to Jesus. We need to pray for their salvation. We need to pray for conviction and conversion. And we need to keep on praying until God tells us to stop.

Thomas Watson, a Puritan pastor from 350 years ago, asked in his book, *Body of Divinity* (Grand Rapids: Baker Book House, 1979, pp. 399–400), *'Why does God delay an answer to prayer?'* In other words, why would God ever keep us asking and seeking and knocking when he could respond sooner? He gives four answers:

- Because He loves to hear the voice of prayer. You let the musician play a great while before you throw him down money, because you love to hear his music.
- That He may humble us. We may too easily assume we merit some ready answer, or that He is at our beck and call like a butler, not as sovereign Lord and loving Father.
- Because He sees we are not yet fit or ready for the mercy we seek. It may be he has things to put in place—in us or in our church or in the world. There are a million pieces to the

puzzle. Some things go first to make a place for the others.
• Finally that the mercy we pray for may be the more prized and may be sweeter when it comes.[40]

God is not slow in answering our prayers, as some understand slowness. Think of it like this: in the third sentence of the Bible we are told God created light: (*'Let there be light'* Genesis 1v3). Do you know how fast light travels or what the speed of light is? 186,000 miles a second. If we could travel at the speed of light then time, as we know it, would cease to exist. Imagine if we could travel at 186,000 miles a second, time would be instantaneous to us; it would be as though we could travel forwards and backwards simultaneously! God is like that. That's why the Bible says: *'With the Lord a day is like a thousand years, and a thousand years are like a day. The Lord is not slow in keeping his promise, as some understand slowness. He is patient with you, not wanting anyone to perish, but everyone to come to repentance.'* (2 Peter 3:8–9)

Ophelia Guyon Browning wrote this poem, which encourages us to continue in prayer:

Unanswered yet the prayer your lips have pleaded
In agony of heart these many years?
Does faith begin to fail, is hope declining,
And think you all in vain those falling tears?
Say not the Father has not heard your prayer;
You shall have your desire, sometime, somewhere.

Unanswered yet? Tho' when you first presented
This one petition at the Father's throne,
It seemed you could not wait the time of asking,
So anxious was your heart to have it done;
If years have passed since then, do not despair,
For God will answer you sometime, somewhere.

Unanswered yet? But you are not unheeded;
The promises of God forever stand;

To Him our days and years alike are equal;
Have faith in God! It is your Lord's command.
Hold on to Jacob's angel, and your prayer
Shall bring a blessing down sometime, somewhere.

Unanswered yet? Nay, do not say unanswered,
Perhaps your part is not yet wholly done,
The work began when first your prayer was uttered,
And God will finish what He has begun.
Keep incense burning at the shrine of prayer,
And glory shall descend sometime, somewhere.

Unanswered yet? Faith cannot be unanswered;
Her feet are firmly planted on the Rock;
Amid the wildest storms she stands undaunted,
Nor quails before the loudest thunder shock.
She knows Omnipotence has heard her prayer,
And cries, 'It shall be done sometime, somewhere.'

When it comes to prayer I find one of the most encouraging passages of Scripture is 1 John 5:14–15 which says: '*This is the confidence we have in approaching God: that if we ask anything according to his will, he hears us. And if we know that he hears us – whatever we ask – we know that we have what we asked of him.*' The fact is, the more we get to know God and the more intimate our relationship is, the more we know His will and so the more of our prayers are answered. Our own personal walk with the Lord and our private prayer life is crucially important, but it's also essential that we pray together with other believers too.

Since 2007 I have met with my close friends and prayer partners, Ken MacDonald and Stephen Abery, every week at 6:30am on a Wednesday morning to pray together for an hour before work. This is a priority meeting for me. We meet specifically to pray for renewal and revival. We pray for individuals; for our churches and church leaders; for missions and missionaries; for our country and government – and foreign ones; we pray for outreach events;

for those we know who are seeking God, and those who aren't (yet); we pray for our Sunday services and for our preaching; for the spread of the gospel and for evangelistic opportunities and so on and so forth. Over the years we have seen many wonderful answers to prayer and this weekly prayer meeting has often been a great source of encouragement to all of us. Now, sometimes, I have to admit, I don't really feel like going (especially in the depths of winter) but I always do, and I have to say I am always glad that I did.

Revival Scriptures to aid prayer:

- Psalm 85v6: *'Will you not revive us again, that you people may rejoice in you?'*
- Isaiah 64v1–2: *'Oh, that you would rend the heavens and come down, that the mountains would tremble before you! As when fire sets twigs ablaze and causes water to boil, come down to make the nations quake before you.'*
- Habakkuk 3v2: *'LORD, I have heard of your fame; I stand in awe of your deeds, O LORD. Renew them in our day, in our time make them known; in wrath remember mercy.'*

I find it really interesting that when Jesus sent the twelve disciples out on mission in Mark 6v7, he sent them out in pairs: two by two. And in Luke 10v1–3, when Jesus appointed the seventy-two other messengers, again He sent them out two by two, saying: *'The harvest is plentiful, but the workers are few. Ask the Lord of the harvest therefore, to send out workers into his harvest field. Go! I am sending you out like lambs among wolves.'* The gospel messengers were sent out in two's. Why? Ecclesiastes chapter 4 provides us with a likely answer: *'Two are better than one, because they have a good return for their work: If one falls down, his friend can help him up. But pity the man who falls and has no one to help him up... A cord of three strands is not quickly broken'* (vv9, 10, 12). Are we better, then, to go fishing or go out into the harvest field in two's or three's – to partner up with other like-minded Christians – so that we can encourage and support each other in prayer and in proclaiming the gospel? I think so. – If you don't already have a prayer partner(s) I want to strongly urge you to try and find the right person(s) and give it a go. Who can you pair or triple up with? Pray and seek God's guidance about this.

Christian prayer meetings create God meetings. Jesus said, *'Where two or three gather together in my name there am I with them'* (Matthew 18:20). But it can be difficult, sometimes, to pray out loud in front of others. I remember the first time Suzanne and I prayed together, shortly after we became Christians. We'd both always believed in God ever since we were children but it was only after our son was born did we finally connect with the gospel and make a personal commitment to follow Christ. I remember after we'd been Christians for a few months, coming home from church one Sunday and talking together in the kitchen about the service. We decided to try and pray aloud together for the very first time. Now when you have been a Christian for a while praying out loud in front of other people can become second nature but as new Christians it can be really hard… to begin with, at least. Normally a husband and wife can talk to each other about anything and share the deepest intimacy but try praying together – especially as new Christians – and it's an uphill struggle with what seems like obstacles and missiles firing at you left, right and centre! That's because there is a cosmic conflict going on in the heavenly realms (see Ephesians 6:12), and the devil most definitely does not want a couple to be at prayer together. Why? Because there's real power when a couple or a husband and wife pray together. Remember what Jesus said: *'I tell you that if two of you on earth agree about anything you ask for, it will be done for you by my Father in heaven'* (Matthew 18:19).

Let me share what happened the first time my wife and I prayed together as fairly new Christians. Feeling apprehensive and after hesitating and stumbling with the *'why don't you start'* and the, *'no, no, you go first'* routine… I eventually plucked up the courage and opened with the words *'Dear God…'* At that precise moment there was a loud thud on the landing at the top of the stairs. Our infant son, Aaron, who had been sleeping, had somehow fallen! Instinctively, Suzanne dashed out of the kitchen, through the sitting room to the hallway and bounded up the stairs, where our son was balancing upside down on his head in the most unnatural way possible! If you can picture the scene: He was upside down, balancing only on his head, and facing backwards into the top of the staircase with his hands and legs all splayed outwards… like someone doing a headstand! Suzanne perceived what could only be described as an invisible force (we later decided it must have an angel) holding our son upright until she was able to clamber up the stairs and catch him at the precise moment that he gently toppled into her arms, completely unharmed! Somehow our infant son had gotten out of his cot-bed! Somehow the safety gate at the top of the stairs had become opened (it was definitely closed beforehand). And somehow our infant son had managed to climb through the stair gate and then fall, almost head first down the stairs! To this day we don't know exactly what happened but my wife and I were very much aware of the Lord's intervention and protection, and we were also very much aware that this incident had happened at the precise moment we were about to pray together for the first time. We figured rightly that the enemy did not want us to be at prayer and so we praised God for His goodness and started praying together immediately after that! Let me say it again, there is a cosmic conflict going on and the enemy does not want believers to be at prayer together because he doesn't want Christian people to discover the power and the answers that come when two or three gather together to pray.

Practical Tip: I always encourage new believers to begin praying out loud with others as soon as possible after coming to faith. I tell them not to try and impress God with elaborate words or with eloquent lengthy prayers, and not to feel intimidated or concerned with what others think (we are not praying to them), but to pray short simple prayers to God from the heart. For my mind, a prayer that doesn't mean much to us is a prayer that probably doesn't mean much to God. Again, to quote John Bunyan: *'In prayer it is better to have a heart without words, than words without a heart.'* I always recommend new believers (or those who are not used to praying aloud in front of others) to start by saying popcorn prayers – one-sentence prayers that you can pop in any time. They can then expand in public prayer as they grow in confidence. Ask yourself: How does a person ever become a prayer-warrior? (Or how do you learn and understand the Scriptures? Or how does a Christian get more involved in evangelism?) The answer is, practise, practice, practice. A good evangelist is always a bad evangelist who got better!

Jesus never taught His disciples how to preach, only how to pray. I once read somewhere that *'when Jesus taught us to pray He didn't begin with 'O omnipotent, omnipresent, omniscient God. Yes, He is all those, but when it comes to us He wants to be recognised and called Father.'* In the prayer Jesus offered in Matthew 6:9–13, famously known as 'The Lord's Prayer' (although 'The Disciples' Prayer' would be a more accurate name), Jesus taught us to approach our heavenly Father in prayer every day and He gave us a pattern for praying. The Lord's Prayer is not meant to simply be memorised and then recited; it is a pattern. Jesus said, when you pray, pray like this:

- Remember who God is, our loving Father; remember God's holiness and offer Him praise (v9)
- Seek God's kingdom to spread and for His purpose and will to be done (v10)
- Ask Him for daily provisions; for what we have need of (v11)
- Ask for forgiveness, and for the power to forgive others (v12)
- Ask for help and deliverance (v13)

This pattern of praying that Jesus gave us puts God's interests first, not ours. The Lord's Prayer begins with God's name, God's kingdom and God's will, and then we are to ask for provision, pardon and protection for ourselves. The pattern of prayer Jesus gave us puts God first – *Thy name, Thy kingdom, Thy will* and puts us second – *give us, forgive us, lead us, deliver us.*

John Stott said he found it helpful for many years, at the beginning of each day, to recite the following trinitarian liturgy, which begins with praise and ends in prayer. I have started to use this myself:

Almighty and everlasting God, Creator and Sustainer of the universe,
  I worship you.
Lord Jesus Christ, Saviour of the world, I worship you.
Holy Spirit, Sanctifier of the people of God, I worship you.
Glory be to the Father and to the Son, and to the Holy Spirit.
As it was in the beginning, is now and ever shall be, world without
  end. Amen.

Heavenly Father, I pray that this day I may live in your presence and
  please you more and more.
Lord Jesus Christ, I pray that this day I may take up my cross and
  follow you.
Holy Spirit, I pray that this day your fruit may ripen in my life –
  love, joy, peace, patience, kindness, goodness, faithfulness, gentleness
  and self-control.
Holy, Blessed and glorious Trinity, three persons and one God, have
  mercy on me. Amen.[41]

Prayer is to evangelism and to ministry like a beating heart is to a living body. Prayer is the most important activity of our lives and it should be central to everything we do – before, during and after we do it. I am going close this chapter with a quote from the famous Dutch Christian and wartime heroine, Corrie ten Boom, who once asked someone this question: '*Is prayer your steering wheel or your spare tyre?*' That's a good question to ask!

Individual or Group prayer challenge: Look to openly pray God's blessing on twenty different people (ideally not-yet Christian people) every single day. It doesn't have to be a lengthy prayer, you might just say, *'God bless you,'* to twenty different people you know or talk to or meet. This is a great witness and it lets people know you are a believer. I have had some amazing evangelistic conversations with people after saying those three words: *God bless you.* And can you imagine the cumulative effect of all those blessings if everyone in your church prayed or blessed twenty different people every day. God has blessed us so that we might be a blessing to others. Let's do it.

An idea for Church Leaders: Prayer meetings are more than just important they are essential. For my mind, the church's prayer meeting is *the most important meeting* on the church's calendar. However, and as we have already noted, open prayer can be difficult and many churches find that their prayer meetings are poorly attended and the least supported meetings in the whole of the church. This should not be so. One church I know has significantly increased the regular numbers attending their monthly prayer meeting simply by changing the name and calling it a 'Prayer Supper'. Each month one of the various house groups takes it in turn to host the supper and prepare a simple dish. People meet for 45 minutes beforehand to eat together and socialise, and then they spend another 45 minutes praying together. This idea has changed the whole dynamics of the prayer meetings because people enjoy each other's company beforehand and are therefore more relaxed when they come to pray together.

Group Exercise: Use these **Covenant Prayers For Revival And Spiritual Awakening**[42] (taken from *'How to Develop a Powerful Prayer Life'* by Dr. Gregory Frizzell), as a guide for your corporate prayers:

1. **Ask God to bring deep conviction of sin, spiritual brokenness, a holy fear of God and genuine repentance among His people.** There will be no revival without these elements and only God can produce them in His people. After all we cannot program or work up genuine brokenness and repentance. (2 Corinthians 7:10)

2. **Pray for deep cleansing, genuine repentance, and spiritual power to engulf pastors and Christian leaders.** Revival and spiritual awakening are extremely unlikely without a mighty move of God in pastors and Christian leaders. Renewed pastors are absolutely crucial to a move of God in our day! (Ephesians 6:14–20)

3. **Pray for God to bestow spiritual hunger in His people and draw them to fervent intercession.** God has to grant people the genuine faith and the fervent desire for prayer. With all our promotion and programming, we cannot produce a genuine prayer movement. (Philippians 2:13)

4. **Pray that God will bring loving unity in our churches and a deep harmony between our churches.** Many churches need healing among members and many churches need to stop competing jealously with other churches. (John 13:35)

5. **Pray for God to fill His people with a passion to see people saved.** Only God can give a genuine burden for souls, until God's people intensely pray for the lost and do aggressive soul winning revival will tarry. Be sure you are constantly praying for many lost people by name. (Romans 9:1–3)

6. **Pray for God to give His people a passion for missions and starting churches.** Great revivals produce an explosion of mission projects, new ministries and new church starts. Only God can grant a genuine passion for missions. (Matthew 28:19)

7. **Pray that God will call thousands into ministry, missions and Christian service.** Many churches are dying for lack of soul winners, teachers and church workers. Furthermore, we can start only as many churches as we have church planters to start them. (Matthew 9:37)

8. **Pray that God will pour out His Spirit like a mighty purifying flood.** Ask God to purify our motives as we pray for revival. After all it is possible to pray for revival for selfish or ambitious reasons. Our motives must be solely for: (a) the glory of God, and (b) the increase of the kingdom of God. We must not pray for revival just to solve our own problems or make our church successful in the eyes of men. (James 4:2)

9. **Pray for a mighty move of conviction and salvation upon communities of cultural influence.** Some key examples are Hollywood actors and producers, government officials, educators, teachers, and college professors, news and media people, talk shows hosts, comedians, homosexual activist groups, and the music industry. (1 Timothy 2:1–2) Provide specific lists for your congregation.

10. **Specifically pray for God to pour out His Spirit in a fashion even greater than He did in America in 1858 and Wales in 1904.** (Ten percent of Wales' population was saved in five months!) Ask God for a modern day of Pentecost. (Mark 11:22–24; John 14:13–14)

Chapter 8

Personal Evangelism:
Living Out Your Faith

'You are the light of the world… Let your light shine before men,
that they may see your good deeds and praise your Father in heaven.'
(Matthew 5:14, 16.)

Jesus calls his followers *'the light of the world'* and He said, *'Let your light shine before men.'* (These are also the words that inspired that old gospel song: *'This little light o' mine, I'm going let it shine.'*) We are called to be Christ's verbal and visual aids shining like bright lights in this lost and dark world. Paul in his letter to all the saints in Christ Jesus at Philippi, wrote: *'Live clean, innocent lives as children of God, shining like bright lights in a world full of crooked and perverse people.'* (Philippians 2:15 NLT) Who were these saints in Philippi that Paul was writing to? Were they a select group of Christians who lived especially godly lives, like nuns or monks in a monastery? No. The word 'saint' comes from the Greek word *'hagios'* which means *'consecrated to God; sacred; holy ones; those who are set apart'*, in other words, all believers who are in Christ Jesus. Saints are not just a few special people: saints are Christians, the body of Christ, the church, *us*. If you are trusting in Jesus then you are what the Bible calls a 'saint' – not like Simon Templar (the character played by Roger Moore in the 1960's and Val Kilmer in the 1990's), but a saint just like St. Paul or St. Timothy or St. Mary. Of course, saints don't really walk around with a 'Ready Brek Glow' a 'Colgate-smile' and a halo hanging over their heads! But actually, that's not a bad description or caricature because saints are people, followers of Christ, who radiate Jesus, who reflect His love and His light to others, *'who shine like stars in the universe'*.

> There is a story told of a young lad who was asked by his Sunday school teacher to describe what a saint was. The boy thought about it for a few moments and then he remembered the pictures of all the saints portrayed on the stained-glass windows in the church. *'I know,'* the little boy answered, *'A saint is someone who lets the light shine through them.'* That's a lovely way of putting it! So then, Saint, let me ask you this: does the light of Christ shine through you?

When people look at us, do they see a difference in the way we live our life, do they see the *'light of the world'* shining through us, and do they see our hope? That's one of the on-going challenges for each and every one of us, and especially so in this whole area of personal evangelism. As Christians, it's like we are on show to a watching world... so we need to live beautifully, and we need to be nice! As the child's prayer goes: *'Lord, make the bad people good and make the good people nice!'* We are meant to radiate the love of Jesus to others and to let the light of Christ shine through us, so that we will be like magnets attracting people to want to find out more. One of my most frequent personal prayers is this, *'Lord fill (me/us) and shine through me. Help me to be so attractive for Jesus that people will see You in me and be attracted to You through me.'* In this chapter, then, we are going to be looking at *personal evangelism:* the nuts and bolts of why and how we should share our faith and tell others the good news about Jesus.

Recently, I was involved in running a fairly large *Alpha Course,* which had been entirely funded by the generosity of our church and which was hosted by numerous volunteers, many of whom were helping out behind the scenes. One evening I said to the guests who were attending Alpha: *'All of us who are involved in running this course have willing given up our free time to do so. Why do you suppose we are doing this? No one is forcing us to; we are not paid to do it; and we are not after your money – the venue, the workbooks, the food and refreshments; everything is free because the church wanted to pay for it… so why do you suppose we are doing this? What's in it for us? What's our motivation?'* I then went on to say three things in response. Why do we do it?

1. We do it because we want to:

We want to share the good news about Jesus because we have discovered it for ourselves and, frankly, it would be so very selfish of us to keep it a secret. When a pregnancy or a birth – or an engagement or a marriage – happens in your family, it's really good news and so you don't keep it to yourself; you share it with everyone. On the other hand, imagine discovering the cure for some debilitating, life-threatening disease and then keeping it a secret: How selfish would that be? The reason we tell others about Jesus is because we have some really good news for all people: As the angel announced to the shepherds, on that first Christmas morning, at the beginning of Luke's gospel (2:10–11): *'I bring you good news of great joy that will be for all the people. Today in the town of David, a Saviour has been born to you; he is Christ the Lord.'*

2. We do it because we are told to:

In Matthew's Gospel (28:19–20) Jesus gave us this directive: 'Go and make disciples of all nations, baptising them in the name of the Father and of the Son and of the Holy Spirit, and teaching them to obey everything I have commanded you. And surely I am with you always, to the very end of the age.' Jesus commands us to 'go and make disciples'. We are to go and make… or go and tell, not wait for people to come in to the church and ask, 'Excuse me, how can I become a disciple of Jesus'? As I have mentioned before, in Romans, chapter 10, Paul talks of his desire to see his fellow Jews accept Christ for themselves and in v13 he states: 'Everyone who calls on the name of the Lord will be saved.' Then, in the next verse, Paul goes on to pose a number of penetrating questions: 'How, then, can they call on the one they have not believed in? And how can they believe in the one whom they have not heard? And how can they hear without someone preaching to them?' How indeed? How can people today believe in Jesus and come to faith; how can they call on the name of the Lord and be saved if they don't actually hear the good news in the first place? We are meant to tell others. Think of it like this: If we didn't follow Jesus' command in the Great Commission, Christianity could potentially die out and the church cease to exist in just one generation! (In actual fact and as we'll see in moment, the good news of Christ has indeed spread and church continues to grow and is larger today than at any other time in history.)

3. We do it because people need it:

There are some 70 million people in the UK and the vast majority are not Christian (regardless of what people tick on the census forms). There is a great need to reach these people with the good news of Jesus. At a recent training conference that I attended, we were told that statistics from the NHS show that there were 43 million prescriptions written for depression in 2011.[43] Some of these, no doubt, will have been repeat prescriptions but even after taking this into account, that's still an awful lot of unhappiness! In the UK there is a crisis of purpose – people are lost and looking for meaning and direction in life. There is also a crisis of spirituality: a spiritual vacuum that people try to fill with all sorts of mystical stuff! And there is also a crisis of contentment or happiness, which 'affluenza' (affluence and wealth) have not been able to satisfy.

In summary, we should tell others the good news of Jesus because we want to, because we are told to and because people really need to hear it. But in telling others there are three common mistakes that we need to avoid.

The first is thinking that we need to have all the answers. We don't. If someone asks us a question and we don't know the answer, or we aren't sure, it's far more credible and better to say, 'I'm not sure how best to answer that, can I look into it and get back to you?' than it is to reply with some incomprehensible response, which has little or no relevance to the original question. Saying that we don't know displays honesty and openness; it gives us an opportunity to go back to the people; and it also provides us with a learning opportunity.

The second mistake we need to avoid is being tactless or insensitive: Walking around the town with a sandwich board draped over your shoulders that says: 'THE END OF THE WORLD IS NIGH' on one side of the A-board and 'TURN OR BURN' on the other; or hijacking every conversation and Bible-bashing people with Scripture passages is not only insensitive, but frankly, it usually has the opposite effect and puts people off. If you have the right doctrine but the wrong spirit, you'll drive more people away from Christ that you'll draw to Him!

And the third and most common mistake Christians need to avoid is being so scared or fearful that we end up not saying anything at all. St. Francis of Assisi is often quoted as saying: 'Go throughout the world preaching the Gospel, and use words if you have to.' People sometimes use the St Francis' quote – about only using words if you have to – as a way of excusing themselves from opening their mouths and talking about the gospel. Sadly, too many believers have applied Jesus' command in the Gospels to themselves: 'Tell no one!' The author and evangelist, J. John, makes a similar point, when he says, 'Unfortunately, too many Christians are like Artic rivers: They remain frozen at the mouth!' We must not make that mistake. Instead we need to follow the W.W.J.D. principle and ask: 'What Would Jesus Do?' Jesus did lots of personal evangelism and He expects us to do so too.

Usually people are fearful of telling others about their faith and what Jesus has done for them, because they are frightened of what others will think or how they will respond. It boils down to a fear of rejection or a fear of being ridiculed or insulted and so they justify their position saying, 'I prefer to keep my faith a private matter!' Well, it's a good job the person who told them about Jesus didn't think the same way otherwise they may not have had any faith at all! In my experience, the problem with people being fearful of telling others is mostly because there has been lots of bad practice in the past, and this has put people off sharing the good news.

But, it really is good news and so how then should we live out our faith and tell others? One man who was asked this question said, 'I feel rather like a mosquito in a nudist camp: I know what I ought to do, but I just don't know where to begin.' Let me share some further thoughts with you:

Let the light of Christ shine through you

In Matthew 5v13–16, Jesus said: '*You are the salt of the earth. But if the salt loses its saltiness, how can it be made salty again? It is no longer good for anything, except to be thrown out and trampled by men.*' This reminds me of the little girl in Sunday school who was asked, '*What does salt do?*' She said: '*Salt makes you thirsty.*' Now, perhaps you and I cannot make people drink, but surely we can make them thirsty – by the way we live our lives. Jesus continued: '*You are the light of the world. A city on a hill cannot be hidden. Neither do people light a lamp and put it under a bowl. Instead they put it on its stand, and it gives light to everyone in the house. In the same way, let your light shine before men, that they may see your good deeds and praise your Father in heaven.*' Let your light *shine*, said Jesus. In other words, let people see the light of Christ in you. As someone has said: '*We Christians should offer living proof, of a loving God, to a watching world*'.

In John chapter 12 Jesus and his disciples were in Jerusalem to celebrate the Passover and some Greeks came to Philip and said, '*Sir, we want to see Jesus.*' To all intents and purposes that's what people are saying to us! They might not quite articulate it like that, but that's what they are really saying: '*Sir, we want to see Jesus.*' Wife; Husband; Parent; Friend… that loved one you long to see become a Christian; *they want to see Jesus!* Love them. Let them see Jesus in you that they might be attracted to Jesus through you.

Jesus said let your light shine, don't hide it or cover it up or under a bowl. Put it on the table. Let it shine for all to see. We are to let the light of Christ shine through us so… Shine Christian, shine! At one evangelistic meeting an agnostic said:

'I wanted to believe in Richard Dawkins but he's not as happy as you are!' He ended up becoming a Christian. As I have said before, there is something profoundly attractive and deeply compelling when we let the light of Jesus shine through us, when we radiate joy and light and life to others. As the saying goes: *'To win some be winsome.'* Make every effort to live a beautiful life and overwhelm people with kindness and love. If we demonstrate God's extravagant and unconditional love with our own acts of charity and kindness, sooner or later people are going to ask: *'Why are you doing this?'* And if someone asks a question like that, well, you can bet your bottom dollar they want to know the answer… what prompts you to do this, what motivates you? *'Let your light shine'*, said Jesus.

Let me share an illustration with you: Years ago there used to be a workman called a *lamplighter*. His job was to carry a lighted lamp on top of a special pole and he would move from one lamppost to the next lighting all the street lamps. I once read about an old man reminiscing about how, as a boy would often look out from his bedroom window to watch the street lamps being lit around the town. As darkness began to fall, he would lose sight of the lamplighter but he could always tell where he'd been because of the trail of bright lights he left behind him; and he could always tell where he was at any given moment because every few minutes or so he'd see him punching holes in the darkness.

Again we're called to be the light of the world; we're called to be lamplighters; Christ's visual and verbal aids punching holes in the darkness; radiating light and shining like a beacon to the lost souls in this dark world; leaving behind us a trail of glowing lights and seeking always to leave a place – or a conversation – brighter for having visited. *'Shine, Christian, shine'* and…

Always be prepared to answer anyone who asks you the reason for the hope that you have.

Some people think Christianity is irrelevant and that the Church around the world is dying out, but far from it, the Church is alive and well… and growing! The Church around the world is not in decline, as some would have us believe. (Actually, it is in decline in Western Europe but there are signs that the tide is turning here in the UK – especially in England and Wales – and 'revival' is on the agenda again of many prayer meetings.) Indeed, around the world the Church is growing faster today than ever before, and in real terms there are more Christians in the world today than at any other time in history. With the aid of satellite television and the internet there are also more and more people coming to hear about Jesus and coming to faith than ever before. The Anglican Church, of which I am a member, has always been good at counting and recording numbers and the Bishop of Oxford, John Pritchard, shares the following recent and encouraging statistics:

- 2.1 billion: the number of Christians in the world – a third of the world's population, comprising Roman Catholics, Protestants, Eastern Orthodox, Anglicans, Pentecostals, and many others.
- 1.1 billion: the number of Roman Catholics, one sixth of the world's population.
- 220–300 million: the number of Eastern Orthodox believers, although some estimate 500 million.
- 80 million: the number of Anglicans worldwide, (17 million in Nigeria alone, which has had to double the number of dioceses in the last ten years to cope with the growth of the Church).
- 70,000: the net increase in the number of Christians every single day worldwide.
- 600 million: the estimate increase in the number of Christians by 2025 compared with 2000.
- 2,000: the number of languages worldwide which have a translated portion of the Bible; 400 languages have the whole Bible.
- In the United States less than 1 per cent claim to be agnostic or atheist.
- Western Europe is the only part of the world where the

Christian faith is struggling. Everywhere else the Church is growing, especially in South America, Africa and South-East Asia. It is estimated there are 10,000 new Christians every day in China.

- While we are about it, let me wave the Church of England flag... 1.7 million: the number of people who attend a Church of England service each month, with about 1 million people attending every Sunday.
- 23 million: the number of hours of voluntary service given by Church of England parishioners each month.
- 1 million (just over): the number of children educated in Church of England schools.[44]

Again, and as I mentioned earlier, what I find really exciting is that there are signs of large-scale church growth again here in the UK, chiefly in the renewal and charismatic evangelical churches, and also in the black Pentecostal churches, especially in the London boroughs where it is reported that there have been over five hundred new Pentecostal churches in the last ten years. One of the largest has 10,000 Christians meeting every Sunday. It's just like Jesus said would happen, the Church is continuing to grow as people hear the truth about Jesus and respond to Him. And Jesus wants us to partner with him in this work, to get involved in personal evangelism and to help grow the church in our own area of influence, one by one by one. To do that, we have to be able to articulate the gospel clearly and be prepared to explain what Scripture says.

In Act chapter 17 Paul was in Thessalonica and he went into the Jewish synagogue on three Sabbaths and reasoned with them from the Scriptures, explaining and proving that the Christ had to suffer and rise from the dead. *'This Jesus I am proclaiming to you is the Christ,'* he said. Some of the Jews were persuaded and joined Paul and Silas, as did a large number of God-fearing Greeks and not a few prominent women (17:1–4). The point I want to make is this; for us to be able to *reason from the Scriptures* – like Paul did – we need to know what the Scriptures say and that's why reading and studying the Bible is so important. The apostle Peter wrote: *'Always be prepared to give an answer to everyone who asks you to give the reason for the hope that you have. But do this with gentleness and respect.'* (1 Peter 3:15) Like the boy scouts' motto: *'Be Prepared,'* we need to know how to answer people's questions, especially the common ones like: What about other faiths: aren't all religions the same? How do we account for all the suffering in the world? (Responses to these and the *Top 10 Questions* people ask can be found in Appendix 1 at the end of this book.) The more we equip ourselves and become conversant with the reasons and arguments for Christianity (known as apologetics), the more effective we will be in personal evangelism. It is only when we are persuaded are we able to help persuade others. I think the last three letters of evangelism (*ism*) should stand for *I'm sold myself.* We need to know how to answer people's questions (even if we have to get back to them) and we need to be able to reason from the Scriptures, which ultimately means, we need to *be prepared*.

Bring others to church with you to hear about Jesus (invite them to come and see for themselves):

We have already said people need to hear the message of Jesus, but in order to do that someone needs to tell them, or at least invite them to come along to church, to see and hear the gospel for themselves. (But don't just invite people, bring them or go and pick them up.) The gospel is good news for everyone and people love to hear the gospel: *Englishmen love the gospel because it is something to argue about. Welshmen love the gospel because it is something to sing about. And Scotsmen… well they love the gospel because it's free!'*

In John chapter 1(v35–42), Andrew (who became one of the first disciples) wanted to find out more about Jesus and so he asked Him, and in response Jesus said: *'Come and see for yourself.'* Andrew then spent the day with Jesus and immediately afterwards he went out and found his brother Simon and told him: *'We have found the Messiah! Come and see.'* Andrew is only mentioned by name eleven times in the New Testament and we don't really know all that much about him. But the one thing we do know is that he brought his brother, Simon *to Christ.*

Jesus gave Simon the nickname, Cephas or Peter (which means the Rock) and it was through the leadership of Peter that Jesus said he would build his church. Now you and I might not be like Peter, who preached one day and three thousand people were converted and added to the church. But we can all be like Andrew who found his brother and said to him, *'Come and see'.* Andrew fished for souls (pun intended) with a rod and line and caught one fish at a time, and Peter fished with a net and caught large numbers of fish! But if Peter was the only person that Andrew ever brought to Jesus, what a difference that one person has made. Likewise, if we bring just one person to Jesus we have no idea where it will lead. Now here's a challenge for you: Why not aim to lead one person to Christ every year and then disciple them. Ask: *'Lord, give me one person...'* If we all did that, in the next twelve months we would double the size of the church!

In his book, *Alpha Questions of Life,* Nicky Gumbel tells the following story, which is set in 1934: A twenty-four year old farmer, Albert McMakin, who had recently become a Christian, was so full of enthusiasm for the gospel that he filled his truck with people and took them to a meeting to hear about Jesus. There was one particular good-looking farmer's son whom he was especially keen to get to a meeting, but the young man was hard to convince – he was too busy falling in and out of love with different girls, and just didn't seem attracted to Christianity at all. Eventually Albert McMakin managed to persuade him by telling him he could drive the truck. When they arrived, Albert's guest decided to go in and he was 'captivated' and began to have thoughts he'd never known before. He went back to the meetings again and again until one night he went forward and gave his life to Jesus. That name of the good-looking farmer's son, who went because he got to drive the truck, was Billy Graham. Since then Billy Graham has led thousands to faith in Jesus Christ. Now we can't all be like Billy Graham, but we can all be like Albert

McMakin – we can all bring our friends to hear about Jesus, to come and see. [45]

Personal or friendship evangelism is much more effective than public evangelism. Even Billy Graham accepts that, and he openly says that the success of his massive public meetings has always been down to massive personal evangelism by lots of other people who, basically, said, *'come and see'*.

Relax and don't try to convert people: Let the Holy Spirit do what only the Holy Spirit can do:

It is not our responsibility to convict people or bring them to faith. That's God's work, not ours. Our job is simply to testify and to bear witness; to preach and teach and reach out to the lost, but it is only the Holy Spirit who convicts people and brings them to faith in Jesus – or not, as the case may be. We cannot convert anybody, although we often wish we could.

An old member of our church, Andy Squire, recently took me to see a friend of his who was dying. Andy desperately wanted to see his friend accept Jesus before it was too late and he pleaded with his friend to see me, which his friend agreed to do. Well, I went along with Andy and I did manage to share the gospel with his friend but it was extremely hard going. Why was it hard? Because as much as Andy desperately wanted to see his friend saved, I saw no evidence at all of the Holy Spirit at work in his friend's life. Now, please don't misunderstand me. Andy's desire was absolutely commendable but people need to be open to the gospel and have ears to hear! I read passages from the Bible to this dying man; I spoke about forgiveness, salvation, eternal life, and Andy's friend was very polite and listened, because of his relationship with Andy, but he made it clear that he wasn't at all interested, and as far as we know he didn't change his mind. Very sad! (Although no one knows for certain what happens between a person and God in the last few moments of life.)

Now I might be an evangelist but if you take the word Christ out of Christian you are left with 'ian' and Ian can't save anybody! Ian stands for *'I Am Nothing'* and if we are Christian that's really what it should stand for: I am nothing Christ is everything. As an evangelist, all I do – what we all need to do – is to look for where the God the Holy Spirit is at work and then seek to go join Him. So how do we know if a person is receptive or if the timing is right or how far along their spiritual journey they are? The answer is that we just have to be obedient to God's leading us, bold in our asking spiritual questions, and we need to persevere, to keep on keeping on.

> Here's an illustration I sometimes use when teaching evangelism (using ½ dozen eggs): A friend of mine keeps chickens and a few cockerels. They are allowed to roam free and so some of these free-range eggs, maybe all of them, will be fertile – if the cockerel has *'cock-a-doodled'* with the hen, that is! How can we tell which ones are fertile and which aren't? We can't. We just have to let the hen sit on them and see what happens! And it's often the same in evangelism: we don't know who will respond and who won't, so we reach out, invite anyone and everyone and see what happens.

Did you know that a hen lays one egg a day but she doesn't sit on the eggs until she has her full clutch of maybe a dozen or more? Then the hen gets broody and sits on the eggs to incubate them. That means some of the eggs are quite old (in egg years!) before they are incubated and brought to life. And it's the same with some people: Gospel seeds may have been sown ages ago but sometimes it can take years before people finally come to faith. Don't ever give up on those you are praying for.

Steve and Lynda have been personal friends of my wife, Suzanne, and I for about 22 years. We regularly prayed for them for years, and witnessed to them whenever we could. We've even been on holidays together; our children have grown up together;

and they have personally witnessed the change that Jesus has brought in our lives. Then about six years ago, when life was pretty tough for them, they finally started coming to church with us. Five years ago they came on a nurture course and we were amazed at just how much of the gospel they actually knew. They both ended up giving their lives to Christ and are now fully integrated members of their own church and home group, and Steve even serves on the PCC. If God has laid someone on your heart never, ever give up on them. Keep on inviting and asking them, watching for that spark of interest… and then fan it into flame!

All believers are commissioned to partner in the work of gospel but it's never a silent partnership. (Actually, a silent partnership is contradiction of terms!) Jesus said, *'Surely I am with you always, to the very end of the age.'* (Matthew 28:20) Our job is to sow the seeds and God will water them, or not, as the case may be. In John's Gospel (16:8) Jesus said, *'the Holy Spirit will convict the world of guilt in regard to sin and righteousness and judgment.'* That's what God the Holy Spirit does and so in that sense we can all relax. We need to know how to answer people's questions but we don't have to win people for Christ with fine sounding arguments, and there is nothing we can ever say or do that will ever stop a person from believing or coming to faith. (We can hinder people but we can't stop them, if God is calling them.) So, we don't need to worry about converting anyone. We can relax (but not in prayer) and let the Holy Spirit do what only the Holy Spirit can do.

Paul said to the Corinthians: *'I came to you in weakness – timid and trembling. And my message and my preaching were very plain. Rather than using clever and persuasive speeches, I relied only on the power of the Holy Spirit. I did this so you would trust not in human wisdom but in the power of God.'* (1 Corinthians 2:3–5 NLT) The truth is, we might be used powerfully in the process of evangelism but again it is only God the Holy Spirit that does the work of conversion. On this point, author, Rick Richardson asks: *'What if we rediscovered the role and reality of the Holy Spirit? What if we saw ourselves as collaborators rather than activists, looking for clues about where God is already at work, expecting God to nudge us, being in an attitude of prayer whenever we are with unchurched people? Evangelism could become an adventure in detection rather than a burden of making it all happen.'* [46] We should be partners or collaborators working with the Holy Spirit. We should go to work where God is working.

But as we look at the lost world around us, it is easy to think that our feeble attempts and efforts are futile, and that we stand little chance of reaching the masses. Consider the following story (which is an adaptation of Loren Eiseley's *'The Starfish Thrower'*) and let it inspire you:

One day a man took a stroll along a beach. As he walked long the man noticed someone in the distance, keep bending down to pick something up and then, almost delicately, throwing it into the ocean. As he came closer the man saw thousands of starfish washed up by the high tide and now left stranded and dying on the beach. He observed a young man picking up the starfish and one by one tossing them gently back into the water. After watching this seemingly futile effort, the observer said, *'Young man, I'm afraid you're wasting your time. There are literally thousands of starfish washed up on this beach and for that matter, probably on every beach along this coastline. It would be impossible for you to save them all or even to make the slightest difference.'* The young man smiled, but there was a determined look in his eye as he bent down to pick up another starfish. Tossing it gently back into the ocean he turned to the older man and replied, *'Well sir, it certainly made a difference to that one!'*

If you will let the light of Christ shine through you; if you're always prepared to answer everyone who asks you the reason for the hope that you have; if you will bring others to church with you to hear about Jesus for themselves; and if you will relax and not try to convert people but allow the Holy Spirit to do what only He can do... then you too can and will make a difference to that one, and to that person, and that one... Let me close by sharing a personal example with you, that made an eternal difference to another lady I used to know:

A few years ago my wife's aged aunt, Daisy Edwards, fell out of bed and injured herself but not seriously. She was taken to hospital and kept in for observation but she ended up contracting the MRSA bug, and died a few days later. Daisy was kept in an isolation room and was unconscious for most of the time. Her sister (my mother-in-law) visited her every day but the killer-virus worked very quickly. One morning just before Aunt Daisy died, I was coming back to my office after dropping the children off at school, and I felt the Lord calling me to visit Daisy in hospital, to share the gospel and pray with her. The feeling was very strong so I was obedient and went.

Aunt Daisy was unconscious and so I sat at her bedside, held her hand and told her that Jesus had sent me to talk to her and pray with her. She remained unconscious throughout my visit but I had my Bible with me and so I read from John 14, where Jesus said, *'In my Father's house there are many rooms... I am going to prepare a place for you... I am the way and the truth and the life.'* Then I said a short prayer of confession and finished with the Lord's Prayer. I couldn't be certain but I thought I saw her lips move ever so slightly when I said, *'Amen.'* Then I left knowing that I could do no more.

Later that evening, my mother and father-in-law went to visit her, for what was to be the last time. To everyone's amazement, Aunt Daisy, was fully awake and sat bolt upright in bed, bright eyed and smiling after just finishing a meal. She told them she had had a wonderful visit earlier that day, and that Ian had come to see her, and prayed for her!

Later that very same night Daisy died and passed into eternity. After what she said to my mother and father in law, I have no doubt that Daisy is now with Jesus in glory. I believe that God brought her back to consciousness one last time; so that I would know I was right to go and tell her about Jesus. Friends, tell others the good news about Jesus: someone may really need to hear it!

Group Exercise: Discuss and answer these questions:
1. List as many reasons as you can why we should be involved in personal evangelism.
2. Why is personal evangelism likely to be difficult?
3. What assurance do we have that God will help us in our personal witnessing and evangelism?
4. What do you feel are the most important things necessary by way of preparation for personal evangelism?

Group Exercise: Leader asks the group this question: '*Who would you like to invite to Alpha or Christianity Explored?*' Then the leader suggests: 'Let's stop right here, bow our heads and ask God if there is anyone He would have us invite.' (Pray) *Lord, I want to ask that you lay upon our hearts the names of those people you want us to invite to Alpha.* (Pause) Then ask for a show of hands if people had one or more names come to their mind. Conclude by quoting Philippians 2v13: '*It is God who works in you to will and to act according to his good purpose.*' This Scripture suggests that if we have prayed and God has laid someone's name of our hearts, then it is God working in us, prompting us to will and act in line with God's plans. It maybe that the time is right and these people will accept your invitation to Alpha, maybe not but that's God's work to draw people, not ours. Our job is to sow seeds and leave it for God to water them. The question is will we ignore this prompting or will we now be bold and invite these people to *come and see.*

Chapter 9

Evangelism: *Sharing Your Story*

'I pray that you may be active in sharing your faith, so that you will have a full understanding of every good thing we have in Christ.'
– Philemon v6

How is it that you come to be reading this book on personal evangelism? Now I am hoping your answer is because you want to be better equipped to spread the gospel and further the work of God's kingdom but can I also suggest that, ultimately, the reason that you are reading this book is because at one time or another someone told you about Jesus. If you are a Christian, then you are reading these words as a direct result of someone else's personal evangelism. In other words, at some point in your life, or probably over a period of time, you heard the gospel proclaimed and you responded. Whatever your story, however God did it with you, He used other people to draw you to himself; He used others to proclaim the way of salvation; to share the gospel, the good news about Christ and you responded, you became a Christian. Good move!

In this section I want us to look at how we, as individuals (and as a church), can be more active in sharing our faith and telling others about Jesus. Of course, there are various and numerous other ways that Christians can proclaim and demonstrate the gospel but I want to focus here solely on that aspect of sharing our faith verbally, through personal evangelism and sharing our testimony. Evangelism is the proclamation of the message of Jesus Christ and as Christians we are each of us called to do what we can and to play our part in evangelising the gospel, even accepting that our individual abilities and opportunities for proclaiming the gospel differ widely from each other. God calls each of us to be conduits of his grace, not cul-de-sacs! We are in a relay race and we are called to pass on the baton, not keep it to ourselves.

So what does it actually mean to evangelise? At the International Congress on World Evangelisation held in Lausanne Switzerland in 1974, a covenant was written and adopted by some 2300 evangelical leaders from all over the world. The 'Lausanne Covenant' answers the question like this: *'To evangelise is to spread the good news that Jesus Christ died for our sins and was raised from the dead according to the Scriptures (1 Cor. 15:3–4), and that as reigning Lord he now offers the forgiveness of sins (Acts 2:32–39) and the liberating gift of the Spirit to all who repent and believe (John 20:21). It is the proclamation of the historical, biblical Christ as Saviour (1 Cor. 1:23, 2 Cor. 4:5) and Lord, with a view to persuading people to come to him personally and so be reconciled to God (2 Cor. 5:11, 20).'*[47] Now that's a great definition, theologically, but it doesn't offer any practical advice about how to actually go about *'persuading people'* or evangelising and sharing our faith with others. So what can we do?

The Bible teaches in 1 Thessalonians 2:8, that to evangelise and share the gospel we must share our lives with others. Following on from this I want to say that every Christian has two stories, that is, the gospel and their own personal story. If someone were to ask us to explain the gospel message, or if they asked us what Christians believe, most of us would be able to articulate some form of response, even if that response is sometimes wholly inadequate or confusing! However, a great way to share your faith with others is to share your own personal story with them, your testimony; the story that God tells about you in heaven. Everyone has a story. Who is Jesus to you? Tell them your B.C (before you came to Christ) and A.D. story (after you accepted Christ). Tell them how things were before you became a Christian, what happened that brought you to faith, and how things are now that you are following Jesus. In the final analysis no one can argue with our own personal experience. That's why a Christian's testimony is so effective; no one can argue with it. I have never met an atheist (or an agnostic) who can say atheism has really changed my life, but every Christian can say that. So tell people how Jesus has changed your life. Tell them your story.

Personal 'relationship' evangelism is much more effective than public evangelism. A recent survey titled, *'Confidently Sharing The Gospel'* and conducted by the Evangelical Alliance; shows that 80% of those surveyed believed that sharing their faith with friends is the most effective form of evangelism today. Whereas only 9% of those surveyed thought that open-air rallies and public preaching, that typified much of the evangelism of the 19th and early to mid–20th centuries, was still an effective way of talking about Jesus.[48] Today it is personal relationship or friendship evangelism that is the most effective way of reaching the lost. So share your life and share your testimony with others and be authentic.

The Christian message is not about pretending that we have it all together and know all the answers. We don't… but we know the One who does! We need to be real and authentic and tell it as it is – and not exaggerate or use persuasive or emotive language to try to 'sell' the gospel message. Let me say if again, it is not our responsibility to bring people to faith. That's God's work, not ours… ours is solely to be His visual and verbal aids. Christians incarnate Christ and others should be able to see and hear that. The best way to do this is to live such a beautiful life that people will see Christ in us and be attracted to Christ through us. But it is God that draws people, not us. Jesus said, in John 6:44, *'No-one can come to me unless the Father, who sent me, draws him.'* When it comes to our personal evangelism we will not be judged on our success or failure, only on our willingness, obedience and faithfulness to do what we can, when we can.

So share your testimony with others. Be authentic, genuine and truthful, and allow the Holy Spirit the time and space to do the supernatural work of convicting and converting. Remember what Paul wrote to the Corinthians: *'My message and my preaching were not with wise and persuasive words, but with a demonstration of the Spirit's power, so that your faith might not rest on men's wisdom, but on God's power'* (1 Corinthians 2:5–6). Again, we can't convert or make anyone become a Christian. Evangelism is always the divine work of God from start to finish. We just have to be authentic, faithful and obedient witnesses. Being real and authentic is key because people relate to authentic people. Author and evangelist, Rick Richardson offers the following advice:

'Did you ever think that the greatest gift you could give to your seeking and sceptical friends is the story of your spiritual struggles and doubts? As you reveal some of the vulnerability and even the darkness of your soul, along with your choice to be true to who you are despite the cost, your friends will listen. Your authority in part comes from your authenticity. (…) Your greatest asset is your humanity. It's your weaknesses, doubts and questions. Most people today are not at first interested in your answers. But they will immediately relate to and identify with your questions and struggles.' [49]

Practical Tip: Use *'Feel, Felt, Found'* to help create opportunity and share your own personal testimony. There is a need to be pastorally sensitive here, but after listening carefully to someone and at the appropriate time, say something along the lines of: *'I understand how you feel. There was a time when I felt the same way that you do (lonely, lost, depressed, unloved etc.) but then I found real meaning and purpose in life. Did I ever tell you about my own journey and how I came to faith?'* When they say no, they have just given you permission to share your testimony! Be authentic and tactful: Remember what 1 Peter 3:15 says: *'Always be prepared to give an answer to everyone who asks you to give the reason for the hope that you have. But do this with gentleness and respect.'* In other words, go fishing but don't blow them out of the water!

My own conversion was something of a Damascus Road experience. Here's my testimony of how I became a Christian, although I hasten to add that I do not necessarily share the whole of my personal story ever time I have the opportunity to give my testimony.

For as long as I can remember, ever since I was a small boy, I have believed in God. When I was about ten years old my grandfather died and shortly afterwards my grandmother came to live a few doors away from us. I would frequently stay over at my grandmother's house, initially to keep her company, and she would often take me along with her to the local church on a Sunday morning. My grandmother played a major role in my upbringing. Of her five grandchildren I was the closest to her and, in fact, from the age of twelve, I was allowed to live with 'Gran' full time, and this caused me to be further influenced by her Christian faith.

I remember one particular incident from my childhood when I was about eleven years old and I had done something wrong (as I recall, I had taken something that didn't belong to me but I can't remember what it was): I felt guilty and I was afraid of being found out, so much so that the following Sunday morning I sneaked off by myself to a local church to pray. (I think it was a Methodist church.) When I arrived the service had already begun and so I crept in the back and sat on an empty pew. I prayed fervently and asked God to forgive me. I pleaded asking Him to overlook my wrongdoing and not let me get caught or punished! And I tried to bargain with God, promising that if He made sure I didn't get found out then I'd never to do it again, and I would always believe in Him. God graciously answered my prayer that day (I never did get caught!) but I am ashamed to say that once the trouble passed, my commitment to God waned! I practiced what has become known as '*parachute religion*': that is, I only dropped in on God when I needed Him!

Growing up and throughout my 20's, my belief in God remained constant but I never read the Bible or looked into the claims of Christianity at all. I suppose I would have called myself a Christian, but I had no meaningful relationship with God and my faith was dry, impersonal, a sort of 'mechanical faith'

– mechanical in the sense that it was without genuine conviction or intimate knowledge of God. As I grew up I'd often pray my 'mechanical prayers' and I would frequently get what I asked for and so that seemed fair enough to me! Very occasionally, if I really wanted something badly enough or if I was worried about something, I would go along to a church service to try and impress God by showing up... but the experience never really did anything for me and I would end up listening to 'lifeless' words (at least they were lifeless to me, at that time) and mumbling (rather than singing) dreary, meaningless songs with a gathering of people who always seemed to be either too happy or blooming miserable!

The truth is I had never really given much thought to things like heaven and hell, sin and death, and Jesus dying on the cross for me. If I am honest my only concern was to satisfy my own ambitions and desires! Over the years, however, I, like many others before me, began to feel discontented with life, as though there was always something missing. I tried my hand at many things to try and fill the void, especially in the areas of business and acquiring wealth and I enjoyed some successes, but nothing ever really satisfied for long.

I can relate very much to the story of the 'rich young man' in Mark's gospel (chapter 10) who came to Jesus and basically said, 'Jesus, I am a fairly decent person. I know I'm not perfect (who is?) but I haven't done anything seriously wrong, and I have always tried to be fair and do the right thing. Surely, I'm okay? What else must I do to inherit eternal life?' At the time I came to faith I was like the rich young man (of sorts), and I also sought out Jesus, thinking I might impress him or win his favour. You see, in my twenties I didn't know the God of love and grace and forgiveness; instead I worshipped a different god, the god of mammon or wealth. I suppose, by the worlds standard I would have been classified as successful and wealthy. Just like the rich young man in Mark chapter 10, money meant a great deal to me. I enjoyed making it, I enjoyed spending it and I enjoyed the attention and the status it provided me with. Although I didn't realise it at the time, money was my god and I was completely lost and hell-bent on destruction.

Things changed dramatically for me in 1993, after the birth of our son, Aaron. Having always thought of myself as a Christian, I wanted to have my son baptised and so I contacted David Rowe, the vicar (at the time) of our local church. David persuaded me and my wife, Suzanne, to attend a 'Christianity Explained' course, so that we could learn what baptism and Christianity was all about and then decide whether or not it was the right thing for us to do for our son.

We went along each week for six weeks and I was extremely challenged and, I am ashamed to say, I gave David a hard time! We eventually finished the course and had our son's baptism service, but it wasn't until a few weeks later – after much soul searching, wrestling with Bible and prayer – that 'the penny finally dropped' and I came to repentance and gave my life to Jesus! The date was July 10th 1993, a momentous day on my calendar, as I shall explain shortly. For months previously, I had fought tooth and nail against making a decision for Christ. I was carrying a lot of baggage (heavily laden) and truth be told, I was frightened of making a commitment. What would it mean? What would I have to give up? I wanted to believe but I was hesitant, stubborn, proud, scared and reluctant, all at the same time. I wanted to accept God on my terms but I knew that wouldn't work and that made me really miserable. I knew Jesus was real and I could sense Him drawing me but I couldn't, or wouldn't let go. I even tried to turn away from Jesus but I couldn't shake him (thank God). It seemed that almost everywhere I turned I saw 'signs' pointing me back to Christ... churches or crosses or Bibles or other Christians, even the branches in the trees looked cross shaped to me! I had absolutely no peace at all and in the end I became so miserable that I just wanted to quit fighting, throw in the towel and surrender. (Some time later, I was interested to read that the night C.S. Lewis made a decision for Christ he described himself as *'perhaps, the most dejected and reluctant convert in all England.'* I felt much the same way!) One evening I went out for a jog to try and escape from my misery for a while. (I realise that what follows is a most unusual conversion experience, and so I have tried always to be discerning in whom I share this with, for fear of promoting others to seek a similar conversion experience before accepting Christ.)

July 10th 1993, started out a grey day, both in the sense that I felt utterly miserable, spiritually, and also because it was very cloudy, which blocked out the sunshine. Early evening I went out from a run to try and clear my thoughts. After I had gone about half a mile, I was running along the outside of a field and I cried out in utter desperation: '*God, help me!*' Suddenly I sensed someone approaching me from behind and I became instantly alert, not startled or fearful, but alert to a presence and also to an overwhelming sense of peace and well-being. I turned my head to look and in my mind's eye I saw an apparition or a vision of Jesus, fully robed, smiling and running alongside me. Instantly I became 'charged' with Holy Spirit and all the hairs on the back of my arms and my neck stood on end. (I had more bumps than a Lincoln biscuit and tingled in places I never knew existed!) I felt a sudden surge of joy and the urge to run faster, and so I did. And Jesus ran effortlessly alongside me, looking directly at me and smiling. No words were spoken and the experience lasted only a few seconds but in that instant I knew that Jesus was calling me to trust Him, and assuring me that He would 'run' alongside me all the days of my life; that He would remain with me always.

For the rest of my time out jogging I was overjoyed by the encounter I had just experienced but as I finished my run and began to cool down, I suddenly became incredulous at what had happened and wondered if it was my mind playing tricks. Just then the dark grey clouds parted and, in the gap, a small piece of clear blue sky appeared and in it a section of a rainbow. I was blown away! Immediately, I recalled that God made promises to Noah and had set a rainbow in the clouds as a sign of His promise. And then I knew the promise that Jesus was making to me and what I needed to do, in order to accept it... Later that evening I knelt on the floor in our lounge and opened my heart in a prayer of commitment... and then I wept and wept. I didn't know why I was weeping; I didn't particularly feel happy or sad, but some time later I came to understand it as a washing or re-birth, like in baptism, and the tears were a sign of relief, on behalf of my soul, that my spirit had finally come home to God. When I eventually rose from my knees I was drenched, washed clean and re-born. And God's amazing saving grace didn't stop there: Two weeks later my wife, Suzanne, made her own personal commitment and gave her own life to Christ (but that's her story to tell, and she often does tell it).

Sixteen months later, on 13th November 1994, Suzanne and I publicly affirmed our faith at a confirmation service presided over by Bishop Maurice Woods. One of the things the candidates were asked to do, was to write a short testimony. What follows is part of what I wrote:

Coming to faith in Jesus Christ was, for me, like the arrival of a long awaited train finally pulling into the station. I knew it was coming and I wanted it to come and yet I was somehow reluctant to it coming. More than that, I was afraid but I didn't know why! I could sense the train coming closer and closer before I actually saw it, but then when I did see it I didn't know whether to shout 'Eureka' or whether to run away and hide. I can pinpoint the actually day my train arrived: July 10th, 1993. It was like I was sitting on a bench on the platform waiting and searching to see if it was my train. Then, as it pulled into the station an announcement: 'The train now arriving on the platform is your train, Ian.' I knew if I boarded the train I would set off on a new journey but my head was full of questions: what about this and what about that? I knew the train was headed for a destination that I wanted to get to but I was afraid to step across the gap and get on board lest I didn't like the journey, or I wanted to get off, or I was being deceived, or my family didn't get on board, or a thousand and one other reasons why I shouldn't do it. I hesitated. Then the train doors opened and I saw, in my mind's eye, Jesus hold out his hand and beckon me to get on board. I remember thinking that if I didn't make that step of faith and step forward across the gap, now, the train might pull away and leave me behind, and then... would it ever return again? Taking that step of faith was a tremendous struggle for me, but as I did so a hand caught me: a hand that has held me ever since.

This is personal story, my testimony of how I came to faith and I now celebrate two birthdays each year: one on 5th May, which is day of my natural birth, and the other on 10th July, the day of my supernatural birth. (I only get one lot of presents though! Shame that.) I always feel it is important to make the point, here, that we do not need to have a Damascus Road experience or a 'conversion date' to prove that we are Christian. After all, you can't remember the day you were born into this world, but if you are reading this there seems to be good evidence to prove that it actually happened!

Some research was recently carried out amongst a number of Christians and the results of which show that most people, 69%, became Christians gradually, rather than being able to pinpoint one dateable conversion experience (which accounts for the other 31%). Sometimes the conversion experience (such as mine) is like a capital V – a sudden change, but for others it is more like a gradual U – as the realisation of Jesus' love for them impacts their heart.[50]

Practical Tip: If someone asks (or if I tell them in conversation) what difference has becoming a Christian made to me personally, I usually respond by saying three things all beginning with the letter 'P': **Peace, Purpose** and **Personal relationship**, and then I expand on each point to show how Jesus makes the difference. (See example below.)

Peace: It is not that being a Christian means that you never worry or that you are no longer concerned with the things of this world. Problems do not automatically evaporate overnight and life does not suddenly become a bed of roses... but overall there is a wonderful and deep sense of peace; knowing that we are reconciled to God and that He is in control. The Bible explains it like this: 'The peace of God, which transcends all understanding, will guard your hearts and minds in Christ Jesus.'[51] As a Christian I have discovered this to be true and I have come to know a 'peace' that I never knew before.

Purpose: Christians know what direction we are heading in; we know where we are going and where our ultimate destination is. 'But what about my life now... what is my purpose; my reason for living?' I don't mind telling you, before I became a Christian I searched for years looking for an answer to that question: 'What is the meaning of life, and more specifically, what is my purpose in life; why am I here?' The Bible is crammed full of God's purpose for mankind but one of the simplest and most accurate definitions I have ever found is the 'Westminster Confession of Faith' (one of the greatest of all the creeds of the Christian Church and first published in 1646). Question one of the Shorter Catechism reads: 'What is the chief end of man?' [What is the chief end... the main purpose or reason for our being?] And the answer: 'Man's chief end is to glorify God, and to enjoy him for ever.' This is the relationship we were born for. We were created to bring glory to God and to enjoy being in relationship with him forever. That is the purpose of mankind, the purpose for each and every one of us. And how exactly are we to glorify God? The Bible teaches that we have been wonderfully made (e.g. Psalm 139), each of us unique with our own individual personality and with our own particular gifts and talents. Our talents are our potential. They are God's gift to us, and what we do with our talents is our gift back to God. Benjamin Franklin wrote: 'Hide not your talents; they for use were made: What's the use of a sundial hidden in the shade!' We are called to use whatever we have, however great or small, to glorify God and enjoy him forever. That is our purpose... but if you try to live without God you are choosing to abandon that purpose! God wants us to know him and to know His purpose for our lives, which leads me to our third 'P':

Personal relationship: A Christian is someone who enjoys a person relationship with the risen Christ, a person who knows God personally. Christianity – that is, true Christianity – is not about rules, robes, rituals or reverends. Christianity is not about religion, it's about a relationship; it's not about intellectual head knowledge, it's about heart knowledge; it's not about religious rule keeping or doing things a certain way, it's about our love for Christ expressed in our willing obedience to follow Him. Religion (like the rich young ruler practised) is spelt 'D-O' and it's all about rule keeping (religion actually means 'rules'); it's all about what I must 'DO' in order to earn God's favour or to get right with God. Christianity, on the other hand is spelt, 'D-O-N-E': it's all about the work that Christ has DONE on the cross to save us. It is by God's grace and His grace alone that we are saved (cf. Ephesians 2:8–9). The only thing we have ever done or contributed to our salvation is our sin!

> Well-known evangelist, J. John said of his own conversion experience: *'The light came on. Even my mother noticed a change in me. Alarmed, she said, 'You have been brainwashed!' My response was quite simple: 'Mum, my brain has been washed. If you only knew what was in my brain before, you'd be pleased it got washed.'* [52]

If I were to ask you, on a scale of 1 to 10 how certain are you of being saved and going to heaven, how would you score? Think of a number. Now if you're a believer and you scored yourself anything less than 10, that most likely means you don't feel worthy enough to go to heaven. And that's absolutely true because none of us are, or ever will be worthy enough in our own right. But do you see that scoring anything less than 10 also means that you are not fully trusting in Jesus; it's like saying that Jesus' death wasn't sufficient to pay for my sin! Scoring anything less than 10 means, in effect, that you are still relying on yourself in trying to become good enough to earn God's approval, his acceptance. No one we will never get to heaven that way!

A Christian, by definition, has to score 10 because a Christian is someone who is trusting in Christ for their salvation. Jesus' death, on the cross, paid for our sin for all time. We are saved. Period! This might sound arrogant or presumptuous but really it's not… it's just having faith: It is taking God at His word; it's trusting in the finished work of Christ! That's why the very last words on Jesus' lips moments before he died were: *'It is finished.'* (John 19:30) What is finished? The price for our salvation: the payment of our sin has been paid in full – Hallelujah!

Those who repent and believe in Christ are saved, 10 out of 10, not because of anything they have done but because of what Jesus has done. Remember… religion is spelt 'D-O' but Christianity is spelt 'D-O-N-E'. It's so wonderfully liberating when you fully grasp this truth. Christianity is not about religion, it's about personal relationship; it's about trusting in Christ! In conclusion, the difference becoming a Christian has made to my life is that I know what it is to have peace, I know what my purpose in life is, and I enjoy a wonderful personal relationship with the Lord Jesus Christ. (My three 'P's again: Peace; Purpose and Personal Relationship.)

In closing I want to say sharing your personal story about how you became a Christian is a great way of evangelising and explaining the gospel, and you never know where it might lead. A number of years ago, for example, a shoe salesman called Edward Kimball shared his personal testimony with another young man in the store where they both worked, and the work colleague ended up accepting Christ for himself. Today Kimball is virtually unknown but most of us know about the young man that he led to Christ in the shoe shop. His name was D.L. Moody, the man who later went on to become the great evangelist and who led thousands to Christ.

Share your testimony; tell others your story. You never know where it might lead. Remember its personal testimony and personal invitations that work best. The words: *In my experience…* (finish the sentence); that's your testimony, and the words: *Come and see,* that's your invitation.

Group Exercise: Break into pairs (preferably not with partners) and share your testimony with each other for two minutes each. The person who starts off should tell the other person how they came to faith in Christ and what Christ has done for them or how being a Christian has changed their life. (It works best if there are no interruptions.) Then swap over and let the other person do the same and share their testimony for two minutes. Conclude by asking what each person learnt and note any feedback. Finally, tell the participants that the exercise they have just participated in is front-line personal evangelism: talking to a friend about your faith. Ask, how hard was that?

Challenge: Now apply what you have just learned by teaming up with a partner and holding each other to account. Agree to share your personal testimony with another person (a non-Christian) at least once a week for the next four weeks. Check in regularly with each other to ask how things are going, to pray and encourage each other. (Share any successes at the front of church. This is a great way of encouraging and motivating others to do the same.)

Personal Exercise: As above but ask a non-Christian friend if they would be willing to listen to your testimony. Just be honest: Tell them you have been reading this book about evangelism and one of the things you have been asked to do, one of the challenges, is to explain to someone how and why you became a Christian. When you have shared your testimony then ask your friend to give you some feedback: What parts were clear? Was anything unclear? This 'exercise' provides a great opportunity for asking spiritual questions and it also allows you to refine or polish your testimony and make any improvements or revisions to the way you share your story with others.

Chapter 10.

Healing and Evangelism:
On the Streets and in the Community

'Now, Lord, (...) enable your servants to speak your word with great boldness. Stretch out your hand to heal and perform miraculous signs and wonders through the name of your holy servant Jesus.'
– Acts 4:29–30

Does God still perform miracles of healing today? The short answer is: Yes, God still performs miracles and yes God still heals people today. Let me begin this section by sharing a recent example with you. Pastor Surprise Sithole (pronounced *'Sit-holy'*) works for Iris Ministries and in the last twenty-five years he has planted more than ten thousand churches in Malawi, Mozambique and throughout southern Africa. In his recent book, *Voice in the Night*, he shares his own personal story about how God called him to be an evangelist, and how miracles and healings are demonstrating the power of the gospel and impacting the church all over Africa.

In one of many incidents described in the book, Surprise Sithole was on the outskirts of a village when he heard a woman screaming and then he heard someone else shouting his name. When he arrived at the scene, a group of people had gathered around a young woman who sobbed in excruciating pain and cried out, *'I don't want to die! Oh God! Please don't let me die.'* The young woman had been bitten by a deadly snake; a poisonous puff adder. Her right leg was already twice the size of the left one and, with the nearest hospital some distance away; she would never have made it in time to receive the antidote treatment! One of the women asked him, *'Will Jesus make her well?'* Surprise knew that Jesus can do anything, and so, in faith, he sat beside the poor girl, put his hands on her swollen leg and simply prayed over and over again, '*Lord Jesus, please bless your child; please bless your child.*' As he prayed droplets of fluid, like beads of sweat, began to drain out of the injured leg and a few moments later the fluid began gushing out and the crowd gasped in amazement as the girl's leg returned to its normal size! She stopped sobbing; the pain had gone and she immediately got back on her feet and walked around feeling fine. It was a miracle! That very same night Surprise Sithole held a public meeting which was full of people who had heard what had happened and who wanted to know more about Jesus. The healing of the young woman demonstrated the power of the gospel and opened the way for effective evangelism, and the end result was that the church in that village grew very rapidly indeed. Yes, God still performs miracles and yes God still heals people.

Surprise Sithole says he's often been asked why so many miracles happen in Africa when they seem to be so rare in the West. Interestingly, he believes it's because in Africa people have a simple faith: they believe what God's Word says and God blesses them for their faith. Whereas in the West, he says, '*people think they are too clever and sophisticated to simple believe and accept God's Word, and so they question everything, including what the Bible says, and this displeases God.*'[53] We will be looking at what the Bible says on this subject of healing shortly, but at this point, it's worth remembering what Jesus said about our need to receive the kingdom of God like a small child (Mark 10:15), that is, we are called to have childlike humility and put our absolute trust in God and in His Word.

Certainly God can and does heal through the use of medicines and the whole of the medical profession, but there is much fear, concern and scepticism surrounding this whole subject of miracles and healings in the church today. Indeed, there is a fine sounding argument saying that we no longer need miracles or the 'greater spiritual gifts' that the Bible talks about, because we now have the full and final word of God. It is suggested, by some, that this is the reason we don't see major miracles anymore. The argument goes something like this: 'Yes it is still God's hand that makes the world go around and the sun come up each morning and yes, God still answers prayer, but we don't see the major miracles such as were performed in Jesus' day and which (seemingly) stopped with the dying out of the apostles, because we now have the full and final word of God; we now have the complete Bible, and so we are to put our trust in God's Word and not in signs and wonders.' It sounds credible, maybe even convincing, but no credible explanation is given to account for the many wonderful healings that do still happen today, and every day, all around us. Nor is any credible answer given to the numerous written records and eyewitness testimonies of major miracles and healings throughout church history, dating all the way back from the Early Church Fathers right up to the present day. (For a sample of some of the miraculous signs and wonders documented by major personalities and Christian movements throughout the centuries to the current day, see the Appendix at the back of John Wimber's book, Power Evangelism, (1985) published by Hodder and Stoughton). Yes, God still performs miracles and healings today.

In the first letter to the Corinthians, chapters 12 through 14, some of the wonderful and supernatural gifts of the Holy Spirit are listed for us, and we are told to eagerly desire them, especially the 'greater gifts' as Paul calls them, which includes the gift of healing (12:31). Why are we to eagerly desire these gifts? The answer is for God's glory, not for our entertainment: because in receiving and using these spiritual gifts we edify and build up the church and bring much honour and glory to God. This begs the question then, if we don't eagerly desire the greater gifts the Holy Spirit bestows, well then, we are not actually doing what the Word of God implores us to do, and we can then end up quashing the Spirit or suggesting maybe that God doesn't do miracles anymore!

It is entirely possible that major miracles, such as healing the blind or the crippled or raising the dead etc., may have dried up here in the West, for a time maybe, but the Bible says nothing about such miracles ceasing altogether or that the 'greater spiritual gifts' are no longer needed or available. In fact, quite the opposite: Jesus said in John 14:12, *'I tell you the truth, anyone who has faith in me will do what I have been doing. He will do even greater things than these.'* Does that actually mean we will do even greater miracles that Jesus did? Well maybe not greater in quality but certainly there has been a greater quantity of miracles since Jesus walked the earth! (We don't know how many people Jesus healed altogether but there are accounts of thirty healings recorded in the four gospels.)

When it comes to *major* miracles, maybe God has chosen to be 'silent' for a time here in the West, but isn't that His right, if He chooses? God, in a sense, was 'silent' when He allowed the Israelites to remain in Egypt for 430 years... but then God sent Moses who performed many miraculous signs and wonders and the people were set free. I wonder if the Israelites in Egypt said God doesn't do *major* miracles anymore! We mustn't quash the Holy Spirit; we mustn't limit God or use the argument of 'silence' to suggest that God is no longer active in performing miracles.

In Matthew's gospel, chapter 10, Jesus sent out the twelve disciples, and He gave them authority to drive out evil spirits and to heal every disease and sickness (v1). Jesus commissioned them specifically to preach the message that the kingdom of heaven is near; to heal the sick; to raise the dead; to cleanse those who have leprosy and to drive out demons (v8). But it wasn't just the disciples that Jesus specifically commissioned! In Luke chapter 10, Jesus appointed seventy-two others with the same commission, to heal the sick and preach the kingdom. It is the very same charge that is given to Christians today; to us: we are to heal the sick and evangelise. The spiritual gift of healing was never intended nor limited only to the apostles. In Mark 16:15–20 Jesus again spoke about miraculous signs that would be performed by those who have faith: He said, *'These signs will accompany those who believe'* (v17) – 'those who believe' means all believers, all Christians; it means us. We have already seen that the New Testament church saw healings as part of the normal activity of the kingdom of

God, and Paul tells us, in 1 Corinthians 12:9, that some people have actually been given the gift of healing. And let's not forget the famous passage in Matthew 28:18–20, known as the *Great Commission,* where Jesus commanded us to: '*Go and make disciples of all nations, baptising them in the name of the Father and of the Son and of the Holy Spirit, and teaching them to obey everything I have commanded you.*' We are told not just to make converts and baptise them, we are told to make disciples and *to teach them to obey everything Jesus commanded us to do*; and that includes healing the sick. Jesus commanded us to heal the sick.

Now, having said that, it is not always God's will that sick people *are* healed. Sometimes it is God's will that people are healed and sometimes it's not. We don't know why that is; it's all part of the divine mystery, but one thing I regularly find to be true is the more people we pray for the more people are healed. The apostle John helps us to get a proper perspective on this issue: In 1 John 5:14–15 he says, '*This is the confidence we have in approaching God: that if we ask anything according to His will, He hears us. And if we know that He hears us – whatever we ask – we know that we have what we asked of Him.*' Again, sometimes it's God's will that people are healed and sometimes it's not. One of the consequences of the *Fall* is that sickness, disability, disease and death are a reality for everyone. And unless Jesus returns beforehand, everyone who is alive today will eventually die as a direct result of some kind of health related issue, even if we just wear out. Again, it is not always God's will that people are healed but that doesn't mean we shouldn't pray for healing. Even when people are not healed, they are often still touched by the compassion and love of God, or by the presence and peace of God, ministered to them through the one who is praying.

Let's have a look at an example of healing and evangelism from the Bible. In Acts Chapter 3, Peter and John went up to the temple in Jerusalem to attend the 3 o'clock prayers, and as they entered into the temple area a crippled man, begging for money, accosted them. The disciples didn't have any money to give him but instead Peter healed the crippled beggar '*in the name of Jesus*

Christ of Nazareth' (v6) and as a result, quite understandably, large crowds gathered to see what all the commotion was about and they were filled with wonder and amazement at what had happened. Peter then seized the moment and preached the gospel, and shortly afterwards another two thousand people or so joined the fledgling church, which had now grown to about five thousand strong (see Acts 4:4).

Peter healed the sick *in the name of Jesus Christ of Nazareth.* What then does it mean to proclaim or to pray in the name of Jesus? Well, let me state categorically that it is not some kind of magic formula to invoke the Holy Spirit and grant us whatever we request! Absolutely not! In actual fact, it was Jesus himself who taught us to ask in His name: In John 14:13–14 Jesus said, *'And I will do whatever you ask in my name, so that the Son may bring glory to the Father. You may ask me for anything in my name, and I will do it.'* Praying in Jesus' name means praying with His authority and asking God the Father to do something because we ask it in Jesus' name seeking to honour Him, to do His will and bring glory to God. Asking in Jesus' name means that we want to pray in accordance with God's will, so that God may be honoured and glorified through whatever we are asking. And as believers we have the authority and confidence to do this. Again, 1 John 5:14–15 states: *'This is the confidence we have in approaching God: that if we ask anything according to his will, he hears us. And if we know that he hears us – whatever we ask – we know that we have what we asked of him.'* Praying in Jesus' name is praying for things that will honour and glorify Jesus and further the work of God's kingdom here on earth.

Let's look at the healing of the crippled beggar in Acts 3 in a bit more detail; specifically I want to address three specific questions: Why did it happen? How did it happen? And where did it lead?

1. Why did it happen: why did this miracle of healing take place?

The crippled beggar didn't ask or expect to be healed; he asked only for money, so why did this healing miracle happen? That's the unspoken question in v12, and Peter provides the answer at the beginning of v13 where he says: '*God has gloried his Servant Jesus.*' That's why it happened: to glorify Jesus and to reveal the kingdom of God. Again, in v16, Peter reinforces why this healing happened: he says, '*By faith in the name of Jesus this man whom you see and know was made strong. It is Jesus' name and the faith that comes through him that has given this complete healing to him, as you can all see.*' It happened to glorify Jesus and to reveal the kingdom of God to all those who were there.

We have already noted that Jesus commanded us to heal the sick and preach the good news, and He has given us the authority to do just that. In Luke 10:8–9 Jesus said: '*When you enter a town and are welcomed… heal the sick who are there and tell them, 'The kingdom of God is near you.'* Jesus knows that people need to both hear that God is King, and they also need to see that God's kingdom is real: that's why Peter's healing of the lame beggar happened, so that people could see and hear the power of God's kingdom. What the world needs today (the West especially) is for the church to return to a *show and tell* message of God's kingdom. People today still need to see and hear the power of gospel and one of the ways of doing this is through healing prayer. Healings in answer to prayer demonstrate a *show and tell* message and provide an altogether different and powerful aspect of authenticating the gospel.

I have personally seen and witnessed countless answers to prayer for healing, and I know many people who have been physically and spiritually healed. In fact, there are so many wonderful stories of God healing people that it's difficult to know which to share as examples.

- One man I know (who is also called Ian) suffered for many years from chronic fatigue syndrome known as M.E., but he was instantly and completely healed after receiving prayer during a Christian event.
- Another man I know (Dave) suffered for years with embarrassing and excruciating pain in his groin area. Doctors

were baffled at how to treat his condition and it became so bad that he began to seriously consider the radical step of castration as a last resort. But then one day in answer to prayer God suddenly healed him and today he is pain free.

- On separate occasions I have known three women (Sarah, Em and Suzie) who for years had each experienced sterility problems, but then after receiving prayer for healing each of them conceived and almost nine months to the day later, they became mothers for the very first time. (Some people would say this is just coincidence but I call it God–incidence. I find the more the church pray for healings the more healings we see happen.)

- As I write this we have just experienced another miraculous healing in our church, in answer to prayer. Amanda Evans (who has given me permission to share her story) wrote this testimony: *'I just wanted to let you know about an amazing answer to prayer in my life. For many, many months I've been suffering badly with severe pain in my knees. So bad in fact that I couldn't even step up from the aisle in Church onto the chancel. Ian had prayed for my knees a few times before but at the last Praise & Healing [Service] he talked about how, at [a recent] New Wine Conference [he'd been] told to pray with more authority for healing and I jumped at the chance of being his guinea pig! At the time it seemed as though I was healed and we told the congregation so but by the time I'd got home the pain was back. The pain had always been randomly intermittent so it was difficult to judge whether any improvement had been made. However, a couple of weeks ago it occurred to me that my knees weren't hurting anymore and that they hadn't hurt for a long time. I have had no pain whatsoever in them for at least three weeks which is amazing! (…) My physiotherapist was of the opinion that no improvement could be made without knee realignment surgery – which he was doubtful I would be offered because I'm so old (charming!).'*

Coming back to the question: why did the healing miracle of the lame beggar happen? The answer is, it happened to glorify Jesus and to reveal the kingdom of God to all those who were present. It happened to authenticate the gospel message; to make people sit up and pay attention; to make them open and receptive; it happened so that Peter would be provided with a wonderful opportunity to preach the gospel, and which he then did.

2. How did it happen: how did this miracle of healing take place?

I would like us to notice something very important in this miracle of healing: Peter says in v7, *'In the name of Jesus Christ of Nazareth, walk.' [Then] taking him by the right hand, he helped him up and instantly the man's feet and ankles became strong.* What I want us to notice is that there is no indication the beggar had any faith to be healed, but Peter did! It was Peter who was the Christian and it was Peter's faith in Jesus that brought about the healing, not the beggar's.

There are several other examples in the New Testament where people were healed, not because of their own faith (often they didn't have faith at that point), but through the faith of others who asked Jesus for healing on their behalf. Take, for example, the faith of the Canaanite woman (in Matthew 15:21–28); a mother whose daughter was in a very dark place and who was suffering terribly. She came to Jesus pleading for her daughter to be exorcized from demon possession, and Jesus commended the woman for her faith (It wasn't her daughter's faith – she was demon possessed – it was the mother's faith that brought about the healing.) Jesus said to her (v28), *'Woman, you have great faith! Your request is granted.' And her daughter was healed from that very hour.* Another example is the story of the synagogue ruler named Jairus (in Mark 5:22–43) who also sought healing for his daughter: again it was Jairus' faith that brought about her healing, not the daughter's. A further example is the Roman centurion (in Matthew 8:5–13) who came to Jesus seeking healing for his servant, who was gravely ill in bed at home. Jesus marvelled at the centurion's faith and said; *'I have not found anyone in Israel with such great faith… It will be done just as you believed it would,' And his servant was healed at that very hour.* The point I want to make again is this: it takes faith to believe that God will heal, and often Jesus uses our faith to heal others and so demonstrate the power of the gospel to them.

The healing we have been looking at happened because Peter had the boldness of faith to believe it would happen. If I am perfectly honest, I don't know that I would have the same boldness of faith to believe in an orthopaedic miracle, such as healing a grown man who was born crippled in both feet. That's not to say it can't happen or doesn't still happen today – I believe it does – but rather, I don't know that I would have the same boldness of faith as Peter did, although I am very open and happy to admit that I am continually praying for increase. That being said, however, and as I have already mentioned earlier, I find the more we pray for people to be healed the more healings take place. The healing of the crippled beggar happened because Peter had the boldness of faith to believe it would happen. And we too need to be bold to the measure of faith that we have. We need to heal the sick and preach the gospel. Thirdly, then…

3. Where did it lead: what happened as a result of this miracle healing taking place?

'The man went with them into the temple courts, walking and jumping and praising God' (v8). The man was a walking talking testimony to the healing power of Jesus and it was evident for everyone to see. Indeed, a large crowd gathered to see for themselves what had happened and they were filled with wonder and amazement. Then Peter – always the evangelist – saw his opportunity and seized the moment: he boldly preached the gospel to the crowd and shortly afterwards around another two thousand or so people joined the fledgling church, which had now grown to about five thousand strong (cf Acts 4:4).

Public demonstrations of God's grace and mercy, such as the healing of this crippled man, create gospel opportunities. We need to pray for the courage to see these opportunities and to seize them by speaking up for Jesus. Does God still heal today? Yes He does. Will God heal non-Christians? Yes, to glorify Jesus… but

God requires us to be bold to the measure of our faith in asking for such healings. (God give me more faith.) In Acts 4:30 the new believers prayed: 'Enable your servants to speak your word with great boldness. Stretch out your hand to heal and perform miraculous signs and wonders through the name of your holy servant Jesus.' This is a prayer we too should pray believing that God will answer and knowing that He will glorify his servant Jesus. Here are a couple of tips:

Practical Tip: When we pray the model prayer that Jesus taught us (the Lord's Prayer) we say: '*Your kingdom come. Your will be done on earth as it is [done] in heaven.*' When we pray this from the heart, we are praying for God's power and authority and lordship (His kingdom) to break into this world; we are praying for things to be done here as they are in heaven. And when we pray by faith and in the power of the Spirit for healing, it's like we are reminding God of this by saying: '*Lord, you commanded us to pray for things here as they are in heaven, where there is no sickness or disease, so I command in the name of Jesus…*' This is actually a great way to pray for healing, but remember God requires us to be bold to the measure of our faith in asking for such healings.

Practical Tip: Before preaching or teaching about healing, or offering prayer ministry at a church service, an outreach event or in a public place (such as street pastoring), take some time out to be alone with God and pray, asking Him for any '*words of knowledge*' (cf 1 Corinthians 12:8) about situations or people He would like to touch or heal through you. I usually take at least 20 minutes to do this, and sometimes much longer depending on how the Holy Spirit leads and ministers to me. (We must never try to rush things. We are the servants, remember, waiting upon the Master to see if wants to share anything with us.) Keep some paper and a pen handy so that you can write down anything that is revealed to you. Deliberately empty your mind so that you are not distracted and don't try to think things up for yourself: wait for the Lord. If and when *a word of knowledge* comes to you, out of the blue as it were, write the revelation down. Philippians 2:13 says: *'It is God who works in you to will and to act according to his good purpose.'* When you receive a word of knowledge or a revelation, be faithful in sharing or following through with it.

(John Wimber once defined *words of knowledge* as 'a supernatural revelation of facts concerning a person or situation which is not learned by the efforts of the natural mind, but is made known by the Spirit of God. This may be in the form of a picture, a word seen or heard in the mind, or a feeling expressed physically.'[54])

Having now considered why and how God often uses healing to provide opportunities for evangelism, I want to spend the rest of this chapter looking at how we can take what we have learnt and put it into practice on to the streets and in the community.

In Luke 4:16 we read: *'[Jesus] went to Nazareth, where he had been brought up, and on the Sabbath day he went into the synagogue, as was his custom.'* From this passage of Scripture we see that Jesus attended public worship services every week, *as was his custom*. It was Jesus' regular practice to go to the synagogue, and it was here that he also often taught and healed people (see for example, the healing of the man with a shrivelled hand in Luke 6:6–11, or the healing of woman who had been crippled for eighteen years in Luke 13:10–13; both of these miracles happened while Jesus was teaching in the synagogue). But Jesus mostly had an itinerant ministry. Jesus sought out the lost. He went looking for them. He didn't sit around in the synagogue (nor would He sit around in a church building or by the telephone in a church office) and wait for the lost to come and seek him. Usually when Jesus ministered to people; when He healed the sick; when He taught and preached about the kingdom of God and evangelised, reaching out to the lost, He went out looking for them on the streets and in the towns and villages; He went to where the people came to fetch water from the local well; He went beside the lake and the fields where people worked; He went out on to the hillsides (where he preached and fed thousands); He went into the village square and to the town gate and into people's homes. In short, Jesus went to where the people were. He didn't sit around waiting for the people to come to him… even though they did, and often in their droves.

If we are to fulfil our God-given role in helping to grow the church, if we are to be effective in our evangelism and reaching out to the lost, then we need to also do the same. We need to take the good news of the gospel (in both word and deed) out to where the people are; we need to go out from church to invite and bring others in to the church. If you want to catch fish you have to go fishing where the fish are! Likewise, if we are to seek the lost and catch people for Christ we have to go to where the lost people are (which is not, primarily, inside a church building – although that is debatable sometimes!). If we spend all of our time with other Christians or tied up in various church meetings then we will never go fishing because we will never have the time (or the energy)! We need to remember that Jesus said, *'Follow me.'* We are to follow Jesus' example and do what He called us to do, which is… to be fishers of men. *'"Follow me," said Jesus, and I will make you fishers of men'* (Matthew 4v19). We are called to be fishers of men, not just aquarium keepers!

Our streets and neighbourhoods, schools, communities, work places and social gatherings are great places to go fishing because they are full of people who have needs. Indeed, wherever there are people there are needs, and where there are unmet needs there are always opportunities for us to minister; to offer help; to love people; to be a friend; to pray with people; to build relationships; to witness; to share our faith; to invite folk somewhere or to something, and so on and so forth. There is so much need all around us, and so much potential opportunity for outreach and evangelism that we cannot possibly do everything ourselves. That's the main reason I wrote this book; to recruit and equip and encourage Christians to get more involved in outreach and evangelism. There is such a great need for more workers. That's why Jesus said: *'The harvest is great, but the workers are few. So pray to the Lord who is in charge of the harvest; ask him to send more workers into his fields'* (Luke 10:2 NLT). Do you realise this is the only time that Jesus asked: *'Would you pray for me? Would you pray to the Lord of the harvest to send out more workers?'* Friends, Jesus knows that we cannot possibly do everything ourselves but that doesn't mean we must not do anything ourselves! We are not to sit on our bums sucking our thumbs until Jesus comes! As I said earlier in this book, God is a missionary and He chooses to use us in His work of salvation, to seek and save the lost. We are to love and witness and proclaim the gospel – that's our job – and the Holy Spirit will convict and convert people – that's His job. If we are going to be obedient and carry out our part of the assignment, as indeed we should and we must, then we need to step out in faith and engage in personal evangelism.

In this final section, then, I am going to share some further thoughts and practical ideas on how we can get more involved in outreach and taking the church out on to the streets and into the community. To help us do this I want to turn again to the book of Acts and explore briefly the story of Philip's encounter with the Ethiopian eunuch, in Acts 8:26–39, and see what we can learn from it. (Do please read the passage to familiarise yourself again with the story.)

You may recall that God sent Philip on a missionary journey to meet with the Ethiopian eunuch, and when they do actually meet up, the eunuch asked Philip to explain a particular passage of Scripture that he was reading and couldn't understand. Philip obliged and explained the passage but, more than that, he also told him the good news about Jesus, baptised him, and sent him on his way converted and rejoicing. Wow! Don't we really want to know what Phillip said, what his strategy for evangelism and explaining the gospel was? Unfortunately, we're not told but one thing we do learn from this passage is that personal invitation and word of mouth evangelism is the way that God chooses to draw people to Himself, including us – we are those who heard and responded. Who was it that told you the gospel? One thing is for certain, you didn't find out by accident! (And if you think that you did, well then, it was a God-incident and not an accident.)

In Acts 8:26 we read: *'Now an angel of the Lord said to Philip, 'Go south to the road – the desert road.'* I want to pick up on a couple of points straight away here: Firstly, we are told that an angel of the Lord *said* to Philip, not an angel *appeared* to Philip. Hebrews 1:14 says *'angels are ministering spirits'*; sometimes angels are visible, sometimes they are not. So Philip heard the Lord's message or messenger... an inner prompting, perhaps? *'Go south.'* The question I want to ask here is are we open, switched on and tuned in to hear God's voice; His nudging, His prompting us to... *'Go and say something; speak up for me'?* Empowered personal evangelism is about our being open to the Holy Spirit; and asking Him to prompt us; to show us opportunities and not to be subtle with us... and then being obedient and stepping out in faith.

As I write this I am mindful of just such an opportunity and prompting I had a few days ago. Not that I explained the good news of Jesus to a stranger, baptised them and sent them on their way converted and rejoicing! The incident I am about to relate was only a fleeting encounter; nevertheless, it was still a work of evangelism. (Remember, evangelism is a process not an event.)

I was in a pub restaurant in Ascot, Berkshire, meeting with some people from my church and I went to the bar to order some drinks. As I recall, I ordered three of 'this' two of 'those' and one of 'so-and-so' and the friendly barmaid chirped in, *'...and a partridge in a pear tree!'* I smiled and commented that she had a fine singing voice and she then responded saying that years ago she used to be in a choir at church. I felt the Holy Spirit prompting me and so I simply said, questioningly, *'used to be?'* The young woman behind the bar then told me she used to go to church years ago but not anymore. When I asked her why not, she said life was too busy and she now had a young daughter and needed to work whenever she could to support her. I sensed a deep longing in the woman's life but I couldn't tell exactly what it was so I said to her, *'I'm a Christian minister... You should go back to church. God wants you to go back to church.'* She looked at me intently and instantly I sensed a spiritual connection and so after a few more friendly words of exchange I said, *'If you don't mind I'd like to pray for you.'* She was very happy for me to do that and so I asked her, *'If you could ask God for anything right now what would you ask of Him?'* For a moment I imagined she might say 'win the lottery' or something similar but instead she said with a sincerity, that possibly betrayed something of her longing, *'I'd ask him to protect my daughter and to provide for us.'* So, there and then at the bar and looking directly at her as she held my gaze, I prayed that God would do just that, and also that He would lead her back to the right church, and back to Himself. The young woman was visible moved as she thanked me and went off back to work.

Now this incident was only a very brief spiritual encounter, and I may never see the woman again, but I felt I'd been obedient to the Spirit's leading and I'm sure the encounter made this young mother think again about her heavenly Father, and maybe even about going back to church.

Coming back to the story in Acts 8, I want us to also notice where Philip went... along the desert road. The desert is a good place to find people who are open to the gospel. It's when people are in the desert that they are most in need and so they are often (not always but often) more open and receptive to hearing the good news. People mostly come to Christ through curiosity, conviction or crisis. Often it's when people have issues and questions that they're most receptive to the gospel (again, not always, but often.) When life is good and everything is hunky-dory many folk have little time or need for God. But when there is a desperate need or some kind of suffering or crisis people are more ready to listen or call out to God in prayer, or allow us to pray for them. C.S. Lewis once described suffering as God's megaphone through which He calls on people to turn to Him. Who do you know who is suffering in some way; maybe with loneliness; sickness; divorce; unemployment; feeling lost or rejected? Situations of desperation can often be an evangelistic opportunity just waiting for you to show up. Desperation welcomes kingdom activity. Where has God placed you? Where is the Holy Spirit at work in those around you right now, those who have questions? Who do you know that's in the desert… lost, thirsty, searching for answers, seeking new purpose or meaning in life? (Stop reading for a moment and think of individuals you know.) Pray for them and then go out to the desert road and meet with them. Look for signs that show spiritual receptiveness. The Ethiopian eunuch showed all the signs of a seeker: he went to Jerusalem to worship (v27); he was searching and reading the Scriptures (v28); he was asking questions (v31, 34, 36). Where is God at work in those around you? Look for the signs: who is burdened, convicted, curious or in a crisis and looking for answers? Identify them, pray and *'go south to the desert…* to meet them, to come alongside them, to offer them help, hope and healing.

That's what Philip did (v27): Philip left the crowds and the excitement and buzz of the thriving new church in Jerusalem. He left the comfort zone of the flourishing church and he went down *'the desert road that goes down from Jerusalem to Gaza'* (which is about a three-day journey on foot), so that he could meet with one lost soul. Why do you suppose God sent Philip, an important key worker and leader in the Jerusalem church, off on a three-day hike to meet with just one solitary individual? The answer, surely, is because God seeks those who are also seeking Him, and God knew that this trip would be worth it! Success in ministry comes yes by yes by yes... by our obedience. Philip knew that much, and so when he heard God's prompting, telling him to go, he was obedient and he went. The eunuch, the Chancellor of the Exchequer no less, a man who had great authority and influence in his own country, ends up being converted and baptised, and then he takes the gospel back with him to Ethiopia and the continent of Africa. Ethiopia (known as Cush in ancient times) must have wondered what in heaven's name had hit it when their born-again chancellor arrived back home, converted to Christianity and set on fire for the gospel!' The truth is, when we are we open, switched on and tuned in to hear God's voice; His nudging and prompting us; and then we are obedient and step out in faith to engage in empowered personal evangelism, well, we just never know where it will lead to.

Coming back to v28: the eunuch was in his chariot reading the Scriptures, from the Book of Isaiah, and the bit in Chapter 53 about *'the Servant of the Lord who was led as a sheep to the slaughter and did not open his mouth before the shearers'*. The Holy Spirit nudged Philip again (v29): '*Go over to the chariot and stay near it.*' Philip was obedient, ran over, and heard the eunuch reading aloud (which, incidentally, is the best way to read the Bible) and then asked, *'Do you understand what you are reading?'* Notice Philip's boldness here: he asked the stranger a probing spiritual question and the eunuch responded by inviting him, in so many words, to *'tell me more'*.

Philip wasn't shy in asking a probing spiritual question and when the eunuch responded by inviting him to *'explain things'*, Philip did... He told him, not just who Isaiah was writing about, but also he explained what the eunuch needed to do to be saved; he then invited the man to accept Jesus for himself and, there and then, he did just that! Now, probably, you and I shouldn't expect to find seekers searching through the Scriptures every time we stop to talk to someone! But if we are open to the Holy Spirit; if we ask the Lord to prompt us; to show us opportunities; to give us boldness to speak up for Him when He wants us to; and to direct and guide our conversations, well then, we are in for a wonderful adventure and a truly exciting journey. Note that I said *the Lord* prompt us; *the Lord* show us opportunities; *the Lord* give us boldness to speak up for Him when He wants us to; *the Lord* direct and guide our conversations. Again, this is God's work, not ours; we just assist Him in it. If we try to convert people in our own strength we will fail. Similar to the story in John's Gospel, chapter 21: When Peter and a number of the other disciples went fishing in their own strength... even though they fished all night, they caught nothing at all, zilch (v3). But when they fished where Jesus told them to fish, they caught an abundance (v6), more than they could possibly handle by themselves! We need to fish when and where Jesus tells us to fish.

The eunuch was reading from Isaiah about the suffering servant and (v35): *'Beginning with that same Scripture, Philip told him the good news about Jesus.'* Philip used the passage as a springboard and told him about Jesus. How would you go about doing that? (Stop and think about it.) One idea might be to use the easy-to-remember evangelistic tool I shared earlier (in Chapter 3: Evangelism: *The Message*): It's really a simple four-word structure or skeleton to help us explain and share the Christian message with others. The four words are: God, Man, Christ, Response: and the message we need to convey is this: *God loves us. We messed up. Christ paid for it. We must receive him.* (If you remember the structure, God, Man, Christ, Response, the rest is just adding meat to the bones!)

We need to remember that evangelism is process; a process that hopefully leads to a conversion experience, but evangelism itself does not necessarily mean preaching the gospel in full to everyone you ever meet. Let me ask you this: if you pray for someone to know Christ, or you invite someone to join Alpha, is that not also evangelism; is that not part of the process? Of course it is. The fact is, some of us are evangelists (cf Ephesians 4:7) but all Christians should be involved in evangelism.

The eunuch, you remember, was reading from Isaiah 53 and after he received Jesus for himself and was baptised, we are then told he continued on his way rejoicing. I wonder, as he continued on his journey if he also continued reading from the prophet Isaiah. Of course, this is pure speculation but I think it's fairly safe to assume that the eunuch would have carried on reading from where he left off. And if he did… well then shortly afterwards he would have read this wonderful affirmation in Isaiah 56:3–5: *'Let no foreigner who has bound himself to the LORD say, The LORD will surely exclude me from his people. And let not any eunuch complain, I am only a dry tree. For this is what the LORD says: To the eunuchs who keep my Sabbaths, who choose what pleases me and hold fast to my covenant – I will give them an everlasting name that will not be cut off.'* This meeting with Philip may have only been a brief spiritual encounter but from the eunuch's point of view, and indeed for the whole of Ethiopia, it was a life-changing encounter.

Philip was open to the Spirit's leading, he was bold in his stepping out and he was willing to take a risk – a huge risk – but this resulted in the eunuch's conversion and the gospel then spreading to the African continent. Let me say it again, if we are open to the leading of the Holy Spirit; and we ask the Lord to prompt us; to show us opportunities; to give us boldness to speak up for Him when He wants us to; and to direct and guide our conversations, well then, we are in for a wonderful adventure and a truly exciting journey. We should understand that God is never offended by us stepping out and taking risks for the kingdom. In Psalm 81v10 the Scripture says: *'Open your mouth wide and I will fill it'* (NRSV). We need to be bold. We need to take risks. We need to step out and speak up. The enemy will always try to hold us back because he doesn't want to lose any territory but the key is to be bold and keep stepping out with the authority that Christ has given us.

As I draw things to a close I want to finish off by sharing some further thoughts and practical ideas on how we can get more involved in outreach and taking the church out on to the streets and into the community. The list of ideas that follows is given purely to inspire your thinking and to assist, maybe, in helping you to plan a strategy for evangelism but, especially, I offer you this list to encourage and stimulate you to be praying for God's vision and leading in your own local setting. Too often in our churches the work of the *'Great Commission'* (Matthew 28:18–20) just drifts along aimlessly – like a piece of driftwood bobbing up and down on the ocean without any rudder or compass to give it direction – and the results are telling are disappointing. At the end of the day what our churches need if they are to grow and make disciples, is on-going sowing and reaping strategies followed by a keeping (discipling) strategy. What is needed is a change in the DNA of our churches to make them more outward looking again, but this can only be done by relying on the Lord's plan, not by making our own, and it needs to start where each individual church is at, not where it is not at! What is needed is a God-given plan, a strategy, and the people to work it. I can't stress this point enough! Church leaders must seek the will of the Lord in planning events of programmes because without the Holy Spirit leading us and empowering us, our efforts, however well intentioned, will always be lacking charisma, power and authority. Please note that this does not necessarily mean more initiatives or outreach events are needed. Ultimately, what is needed is everything else contained in this book before reaching this point, not simply more ideas or initiatives.

I am not going to spend any time elaborating on these ideas (I will leave that to you) and I am sure you can come up lots of other ways to get involved in evangelism in your local setting and taking your church out on to the streets and into the community. What follows is intended to whet your appetite and stimulate your thinking and prayers. Do please remember, we cannot do everything but we must not do nothing!

Now it's time to stop reading about evangelism and get on with doing it. In the name of Jesus, go... go and make disciples of all nations.

12 Ideas to Take the Church out on to the Streets and into the Community

1. Street evangelism: When seeking to pray for people on the streets or in a public place one of the hardest challenges is

knowing how to approach people. Here's an idea I have tried and that works well: Change £5 into 20p, 10p and 5p pieces. Put the loose coins on a tray and make up a sign saying, *'FREE CHANGE'*. Then give the money away to passers-by. (People only took one or two coins… but most did not want to take any money. They just wanted to find out what was going on). Tell them you are from 'the church' and you are giving away free change because you want to ask people this question: *'If you could change one thing in your own life right now, what would it be?'* However they answer offer to pray for *'whatever'* there and then. (Depending on what they say, you may have to re-package things slightly!)

2. I have had a lollipop sign made up with the words PRAYER STOP on it, similar in design to the 'STOP – CHILDREN CROSSING' sign that most people are familiar with (from outside schools). I have used this several times in various settings and have been able to witness and pray with lots of people.

3. Chris Duffett (president of the Baptist Union of Great Britain in 2012–2013) shares these similar ideas, some of them quite outlandish but if you have the personality to pull it off, why not…

    *   Use a prayer sofa (in a public place) with a sign beside it saying: 'I WILL LISTEN.'
    *   Hold up sign saying, 'FREE HUGS' – (after hugging say, 'God loves you'.)
    *   The Red Carpet Treatment: A strip of red carpet is laid on the ground, with quality rope dividers and poles running parallel along both sides to form a walkway. Then as inquisitive people (shoppers) walk down it, Chris Duffett and his colleagues whoop, cheer and clap and say… *'You are a VIP in God's eyes'*.
    *   Use a homemade maze (made out of a large green tarpaulin with duct tape to create the maze). At the centre of the maze is a treasure chest and when you look inside there is a mirror with a message underneath saying, *'You*

are the real treasure in God's eyes. Christ gave his life for you.'
- Postcards from heaven: Give away postcards with scriptures verses written on them.
- Choose 9 different kinds of fruit to give away, each labelled with 1 of the 9 different spiritual gifts listed in Galatians 5v22–23. People choose a particular fruit and they get to eat some love, joy peace etc. (And receive a prayer of blessing for the same.)

4. Have a MISSION MONTH. There are countless ways to plan outreach or social events to invite guests to and to build relationships. Here are some more active ideas to get you thinking: Quad biking; Canoe or Rowing Boat Hire; 5-A-Side Football; Basketball; Indoor Bowls; Table Tennis; Golf day or Pitch & Put; Water Polo; Ten Pin Bowling; Scalectrix & Supper; Curry Night; Dads & Lads Bike Ride; Paint balling; Laser Quest; Go-Karting; Picnics or B-B-Q; Camping; Walks or Rambling; Watching the match on Big Screen; Pub Night – Grill a Christian event; Men's or Women's Breakfasts with Guest Speaker; Fishing Trip; Skittles Evening; Barn Dance; Quiz Nights and so on and so forth. For more ideas and resources, especially for men, go to the organisation Christian Vision for Men www.cvmen.org.uk or Christians in Sport (speakers) www.christiansinsport.org.uk

5. Partner with the organisation Christians Against Poverty (CAP). Make a difference in your local community with the CAP Money Course and see lives changed through opening a CAP Debt Centre or a Job Club. Find out more at www.capuk.org/partnership

6. Get involved with a local food bank or start one at your church. – A while ago I spent some limited time as a volunteer with ReadiFood (part of FAITH Christian Group) in Reading, delivering emergency food parcels to families and individuals in need. This is often life impacting on those who receive a parcel and it's a wonderful witness to the love of Christ. The Christian charity I worked with put leaflets in the food

parcels explaining the motive behind their work – sharing the love of Christ in a practical way – and everyone got a free copy of one of the gospels in their second food drop. This is effective, low-key but high visual impact evangelism, in word and deed, the best kind of witness. (After receiving an emergency food parcel and reading the leaflet, I wonder how many people have thought of God and prayed, maybe for the first time, to thank Him for His provision.)

7. Get your church involved with the Back To Church Sunday initiative. Find out more at www.backtochurch.co.uk

8. Introduce a 'Community Prayer Drop'. This basically involves regularly delivering invitational church literature (maybe in the form of a newsletter) to every home in the area and praying over every home at the same time. (For an example of how this works in practice and to see the sort of results that can be achieved see the 'Practical Tips' section at the end of Chapter 5, Evangelism: And the Church.)

9. Get involved with the Jesus Video Project – offering households in the community the story of Jesus on DVD (the most watched film in history). Details for the UK can be found here www.agape.org.uk/Ministries/JesusVideoProject

10. Prayer Visiting (60% of people pray – even more are glad when people pray for them). The following example is taken from the Emmaus Course: 'Three churches in a village worked together to 'prayer visit'. A letter was delivered to each house in an area explaining that the church were praying for the area. The letter stated that someone would call later to see if there was anything they wanted prayer for. Their streets would be prayed for the following Sunday, along with their requests (unless they asked for confidentiality). When visited, nearly half had something they wanted prayer for. Only 10% were not interested. The rest thought it was a good idea. Often the visit led to long chats as people unburdened themselves or shared their happiness. Prayer visiting shows that the Church:
    • Cares for people who are not churchgoers.
    • Believes in prayer and has a spiritual basis.

- Is not after your money (any gifts should be politely refused).[55]

11. Establish a mother and toddler group (a great networking and sowing the seed project)… once the group is established, say six months, this can lead on to a monthly parenting course (relationship building) and then an enquirer's course (reaping). Sowing and reaping are not done in the same season.

12. There should be regular evangelistic events at church, at least every term. Alpha, Christianity Explored or similar nurture courses should also be run regularly. Plan and put these courses in the diary at the beginning of each year. Make it easy to invite people. Involve the whole church: get them thinking who to invite; encourage prayer and fasting.

'Now to him who is able to do immeasurably more than all we can ask or imagine, according to his power at work within us, to him be glory in the church and in Christ Jesus throughout all generations, for ever and ever! Amen.' (Ephesians 3v20–21)

Appendix 1.

Responses to the Top 10 Questions about Christianity

'*Be wise in the way you act towards outsiders; make the most of every opportunity. Let your conversation be always full of grace, seasoned with salt, so that you may know how to answer everyone.*'
Colossians 4v5–6

Sometimes we need to discern the difference between someone who doesn't understand Christianity but who wants to believe and someone who doesn't understand because they refuse to believe. Throughout this book I have continually made the point that no matter what we do we cannot make people believe and come to faith in Christ... only God can do that. In John's gospel, chapter 6, Jesus himself made that clear when He said: '*All the Father gives me will come to me (v37)... No one can come to me unless the Father who sent me draws him (v44)... Everyone who listens to the Father and learns from him comes to me (v45)... No-one can come to me unless the Father has enabled him (v65).*' Personally, then, I see little point in wasting much time or effort in trying to answer questions or convince people about the truths of Christianity if they refuse to believe (unless, of course, it is in a public setting where there are others in the audience that God may be touching and drawing to Jesus.) To find out if someone is either a 'moth' or a 'mole' – moths are attracted to the light but moles are repelled by the light – you could ask them plainly: '*If I could answer all of your questions to your complete satisfaction, would you believe and follow Christ; would you like to have faith and know God personally?*' In any event, and however people react to the Christian faith, we must always be gracious in the way we respond to any criticisms, comments or questions, so... Let your conversation be always full of grace, seasoned with salt, so that you may know how to answer everyone. (Col. 4v6)

This section gives some suggested approaches to answering the most frequently asked questions that people ask:

1. **How can I know God exists?**
   - Evidence: The argument from creation – the world and design.
   - Evidence: The argument from human life – personality, morality and conscience.
   - Evidence: The fact of Jesus Christ – that God came to earth in the person Jesus. (People sometimes ask: *'Have you ever seen God?'* We can say: *'No, but I may very well have done if I'd been around 2000 years ago!'*)
   - Re-read Chapter 2: *Pre-Evangelism*: Preparing Ground and Sowing Seeds (p.29)
   - The Bible teaches that God has set eternity in the hearts of men (Ecclesiastes 3v11). We are born with eternity in our hearts; with a deep desire for meaning and to be more than just dust which returns to dust.
   - Is it not reasonable to suggest that the existence of hunger in your life presupposes the existence of something that will satisfy your hunger; that is, food? Around the world there are millions of people today who are spiritually hungry and searching for God. Is it not also reasonable to suggest, then, that the existence of spiritual hunger presupposes the existence of God who satisfies our spiritual hunger?

2. **Hasn't science disproved Christianity?**
   - The intricate precision and fine-tuning of the universe makes more sense if there is a God than if there isn't.
   - Science and Christianity are at not necessarily at odds with one another. Many believe that they complement each other. The fact is, there are many scientists who are

Christians. Science only ever seeks to answer the question, 'how?' but Christianity never attempts to answer that question: Christianity seeks to answer the question 'who' not 'how'.

- Sir Isaac Newton, famous for discovering the law of gravity, said, *'In the absence of any other proof, the thumb alone would convince me of God's existence.'*
- Avoid getting drawn into a scientific debate about evolution or carbon dating. (Evolution is a theory not a fact; evolution is a description but that doesn't rule out God's involvement.) Discuss the facts regarding Jesus.
- Re-read Chapter 2: *Pre-Evangelism*: Preparing Ground and Sowing Seeds (p.29), especially the section: Evidence No.1: The Argument From Creation.

3. **What about all the suffering in the world?**
   - People sometimes ask this as a red herring or to deride faith. Find out if it is a genuine concern.
   - Many who ask this question have suffered themselves in some way, but if there is no God then why do we even care or get upset or feel injustice at suffering? If this is just the way things are then why does it bother us so much?
   - Most Christians can give a reasonable response to the question of why suffering exists. When we have done so, we can then turn the question round, go on the offensive and ask the questioner, 'how they would they explain the reason for all the suffering in the world'. (We mustn't shy away from turning a difficult question back on the questioner. Jesus often did that and to great effect.)
   - We do not know for certain why God allowed evil and suffering to enter into the world but that doesn't mean God isn't concerned about it. He is.

4. **Why does God allow people get sick?**
   - All suffering, ultimately, is the consequence of our fallen world and our fallen nature (cf. Romans 8v18–25). In our

fallen world – no longer perfect because of sin – sickness
and disease are commonplace, and the causes are varied
and often multiple (e.g. poor diet; inadequate nutrition;
neglect; lack of exercise; coming into contact with a virus
etc.).

- Sometimes sickness can be as a direct result of sinful
behaviour (e.g. immorality, greed, violence, drunkenness,
substance abuse etc.)
- Sometimes sickness is even a direct attack by Satan (look at
Job or Paul's thorn in the flesh).
- Sometimes God uses suffering to discipline his children
and strengthen them (cf. Romans 5v3–5, Hebrews 12v7–
11)

5. **If God really exists why doesn't he intervene and do
something to end suffering and stop all the evil in the
world?**
- Re-read Chapter 10: *Healing and Evangelism: On the Streets
and in the Community* (p.173)
- God has done something about it, He sent Jesus.
- God is doing something about it (God is not inactive or
impotent), and one day soon…
- God will do something about it, conclusively (when Jesus
returns).

6. **How do we know the Bible is reliable? (Isn't the Bible
full of contradictions?)**
- For evidence see 'Chapter 6: The Bible and Evangelism'
(p.103), especially the section: How God has revealed
Himself to us through the Bible (p.108).
- We should understand that we are not called to believe
in a book, as such, we called to believe in Christ Jesus, as
revealed to us in and through the book.
- One powerful way of challenging someone's doubts about
the Bible's truth is to read out to them Isaiah 53:4–6, and
to ask: Who is that talking about? When they admit it

sounds very much like Jesus, turn your Bible around and say to them: 'This was written 700 years before He was born!' (From *explore* Bible notes)

7. **What about all the other religions? (Don't they all lead to God; aren't they all just different paths up the same mountain?)**
   - People sometimes say that just as there are many different paths that lead to the top of a mountain, so there are many different religions and routes to God. God, however, says something very different: God says there are many mountains but only one of them leads to life with Him.
   - The only way to really know how to get to the top of the mountain is to have been there! Jesus is not a prophet come to Earth to find God. He is God come to find us.
   - Stay away from making negative remarks about other religions. Don't pull other religions down just lift Jesus up. Talk about Jesus' uniqueness. (Read *Searching Issues,* Chapter 2, written by Nicky Gumbel.)
   - Being sincere does not necessarily mean someone is right; people can be sincere and still be sincerely wrong. Here are a couple of helpful quotes:

In his book, *It Makes Sense,* Stephen Gaukroger writes: 'If we take the five most commonly thought of as the world's major religions, a brief examination reveals mammoth differences between them. Hinduism believes in many gods; Islam is absolutely insistent there is only one. Buddhism is silent about the nature of God or even whether he exists; Judaism describes his character in detail. Christians believe that in this world there is only one life and one death for each individual; Buddhists believe that we keep returning to this world in a series of multiple reincarnations... Christians, in opposition to all the others, say salvation cannot be earned by doing anything; you receive it as a gift. It's only possible to believe that 'all roads lead to God' if we remain ignorant about these different religions and their views of God. All religions do not lead to the same point any more than all aeroplanes from Heathrow go to New York![56]

Philip Yancey, in *The Jesus I Never Knew*, writes: 'Jesus' audacious claims about himself pose what may be the central problem of all history, the dividing point between Christianity and other religions. Although Muslims and, increasingly, Jews respect Jesus as a great teacher and prophet, no Muslim can imagine Mohammed claiming to be Allah any more than a Jew can imagine Moses claiming to be Yahweh. Likewise, Hindus believe in many incarnations but not one Incarnation, while Buddhists have no categories to conceive of a sovereign God becoming a human being. (…) It is an incontestable fact of history that Jesus' followers, the same ones who were scratching their heads over his words at the Last Supper, a few weeks later were proclaiming him as the 'Holy and Righteous One,' the 'Lord,' the 'author of life.' By the time the Gospels were written they regarded him as the Word who was God, through whom all things were made.'[57]

8. **What about those people who have never heard about Jesus or those were born before Jesus came?**
    - We can trust that God will be fair and just and always do what is right (cf. Genesis 18v25)
    - God will judge people on what they know, not on what they don't know.
    - Scripture indicates that everyone has received some revelation from creation to know that God exists (cf Romans 1:18–20)
    - The question now is really, not about others, but what about you?

In responding to this question Stephen Gaukroger writes: 'When slavery was abolished in the British Empire in 1833, thousands of people in Africa were made safe from the threat of captivity and abduction to the West Indies and the Americas. Many of them knew nothing about the British Government and even less about the act of Parliament that guaranteed their freedom! Despite this ignorance, they enjoyed the freedom the act obtained for them. In the same way, any person anywhere who is really sorry for the wrong in their lives and throws themselves completely on God's mercy for their salvation can enjoy the benefits of the Christian message, even though they do not know the facts about Jesus' death and resurrection... I may, for example, get my wife a gift on the strength of a pay rise I have been promised. She experiences the benefit of the increase before I get the money because I know it is coming! Similarly, God chose to accept people in Old Testament times on the strength of what he knew was coming, in response to their faith.[58]

9. **I can't believe in a God who sends people to hell. (Why would God send people to hell?)**
   - God doesn't send people to hell. People make that choice themselves. There is only one way to go hell and that is to reject the one way to heaven. Jesus came to save people from hell.
   - God doesn't want anyone to go to hell (see 1 Timothy 2v4, 2 Peter 3v9b)

10. **Isn't the church just full of hypocrites?**
   - Well, yes it is, so one more won't be a problem, why don't you come and join us?
   - In a sense, we are all hypocrites because we want to live in a way that pleases God but we all fail; we can't do it, at least not all the time. The church is not full of perfect people; it's full of imperfect people who are seeking to please God.
   - It is sad but true that many wrong and scandalous things have happened in the church and this can portray the church in a bad light. But we mustn't judge the whole of

the church on the wrong actions of a few. There are a few football hooligans who behave wrongly but that doesn't mean all football fans or the game itself is wrong. It is the same with the church.

- Christianity is about a relationship with Christ. In ancient Greece actors in a play were called hypocrites because they wore a mask. And Jesus wants us to know that God isn't interested in a mask of holiness, but the real thing.

The suggested answers, here, are designed as an aide memoire but you should get to grips with knowing how to respond to these and other such questions by reading up on the subject. A list of recommended reading material follows:

Appendix 2.

Recommended Reading

A list of further recommended reading covering apologetics, evangelism, healing, prayer and preaching:

The Bible

Alpha Questions of Life, Nicky Gumbel (Kingsway)

Christianity Explored, Rico Tice & Barry Cooper (Good Book Company)

Emmaus the way of faith – Stage 1: Contact (Church House Publishing)

Experiencing Revival, Charles Finney (Whitaker House)

For What It's Worth, Simon Guillebaud (Monarch)

Hosting the Presence, Bill Johnson (Destiny Image)

How to Give Away Your Faith, Paul E. Little (IVP)

I Believe in Preaching, John Stott ((Hodder & Stoughton)

It Makes Sense, Stephen Gaukroger (Scripture Union)

Is Anyone There, David Watson (Hodder & Stoughton)

Learning to Heal, John Coles (Authentic Media)

Lost For Words, James Lawrence (Bible Reading Fellowship)

More, Simon Ponsonby (Victor)

Out of the Saltshaker & into the World, Rebecca Manley Pippert (IVP)

Permission Evangelism, Michael L. Simpson (NexGen)

Power Evangelism, John Wimber (Hodder & Stoughton)

Preaching and Preachers, Dr Martyn Lloyd-Jones (Hodder & Stoughton)

Prophetic Evangelism, Mark Stibbe (Authentic Media)

Purpose Driven Church, Rick Warren (Zondervan)

Re imagining Evangelism, Rick Richardson (Scripture Union)

Saving Eutychus, Gary Miller & Phil Campbell (Matthias Media)

Searching Issues, Nicky Gumbel (Kingsway)

The Essential Guide to Healing, Bill Johnson, Randy Clark (Chosen Books)

When Heaven Invades Earth, Bill Johnson (Treasure House)

Why Believe The Bible? John Blanchard (Evangelical Press)

Notes

Chapter 1

1. http://www.htb.org.uk/about–htb/related–churches
2. Michael L. Simpson, 2003, *Permission Evangelism,* Colorado Springs: NexGen, p.51
3. Bill Johnson and Randy Clark: 2011, *The Essential Guide to Healing,* Minnesota: Chosen Books, p.137
4. Source: *Talking Of God* course from the Methodist Church. Cf. http://www.methodist.org.uk/downloads/ev-talkingofgod-leadernotes-060411.pdf

Chapter 2

5. *Source: Is Anyone There* by David Watson, 1979, London: Hodder & Stoughton, p27.
6. Ibid p27
7. Source: Adapted from Life Application Bible (NIV) commentary notes on Genesis 1:1.
8. Michael Green, *After Alpha,* 2004, Eastbourne, NexGen, p.40.
9. John Chapman, *A Fresh Start,* 1997, London: Matthias Media, p126.
10. C.S. Lewis, 1974, *Mere Christianity,* London: Fount, p52

Chapter 3

11. Common Worship: Services & Prayers for the Church of England, London: Church House Publishing (2000), p.xi
12. Mark 1:15 (NIV)
13. Luke 19:10 (NIV)
14. Paul E. Little: *Know What You Believe* (2008 edition), Illinois: IVP Books, chapter 3 pages.54–66
15. Printed in *The Word For Today* devotional (30/5/09)
16. Adapted from H & R Blackaby and C King, *Experiencing God:* 2008, B&H Publishing, Nashville, Tennessee, p3–4
17. Author unknown. Source: http://bible.org/illustration/john–316 (accessed 14/12/12/)

Chapter 4

18. The Catechism, *Book of Common Prayer,* (1662), Cambridge University Press Standard Edition, p.294
19. Calvin: *Institutes of the Christian Religion*, Ed. McNeill, John T., 1960, London SCM Press, Book IV, Chapter XVI pp.1326–7
20. Nicky Gumbel, *Alpha Questions of Life,* 2007 edition, Eastbourne: Kingsway Communications, p.123.
21. Tom Wright, 2004, *LUKE for EVERYONE,* London: SPCK, p.169.

Chapter 5

22. Mark Stibbe, 2004, *Prophetic Evangelism,* Milton Keynes: Authentic Media, p.176
23. http://www.unlockingthegrowth.com/card/
24. Stephen Gaukroger, 2004, *First Steps: The handbook to following Christ,* Milton Keynes: Scripture Union, p.71
25. Sourced partly from Kim Hawtrey of Impact Evangelism and published in *Six Steps To Talking About Jesus* (study guide): 2006, Matthias Media, NSW Australia, p38–39

Chapter 6

26. Cited in *Explore Bible notes* 24/6/2009, published by The

Good Book Company, New Malden, Surrey.

27. Paul E. Little, 2003, *Know What You Believe,* Illinois: IVP Books, p.16

28. Source: Article by J.N. Birdwell, *'Canon Of The New Testament'* published in *The New Bible Dictionary,* 1962, London: Inter-Varsity Press, p.194–197

29. Source: Bible Society (online: biblesociety.org.uk)

30. Cited in *Why Believe The Bible?* by John Blanchard, 2004, Darlington: Evangelical Press, p.13

31. Ibid. p.25

32. Ibid. p.28

33. Cited in *Is Anyone There?* by David Watson, 1979, London: Hodder and Stoughton, p.29

34. Charles H. Spurgeon, 2000, *Morning By Morning*, Florida: Bridge-Logos Publishers, (Devotional for September 1st.)

35. Nicky Gumbel, 1993, *Alpha Questions of Life,* Eastbourne: Kingsway Communications, p.93

36. Rick Richardson, 2007, *Re-imagining Evangelism,* Milton Keynes: Scripture Union, p.120

37. *Explore* is published by The Good Book Company - www.thegoodbook.co.uk

Chapter 7
38. Ronald Dunn, *Don't Just Stand There…Pray Something,* p.16

39. Blackaby & King, *Experiencing God,* 2008 edition, Nashville Tennessee: B&H Publishing, p.126

40. Source: http://www.desiringgod.org/ResourceLibrary/Sermons/ByDate/1996/950_When_God_Says_Not_Now

41. John Stott, 2006, *Through The Bible The Year,* Abingdon Oxon: Candle Books, p296

42. Various adaptations freely available on the Internet. This version sourced from:
http://www.graceb3.org/wp-content/uploads/2010/10/TEN-PRAYERS-FOR-REVIVAL-AND-SPIRITUAL-AWAKENING.pdf

Chapter 8

43. Source: Cited by Martin Cavendar of ReSource, at the Berkshire Archdeaconry training day 'Confidence in Discipleship' 01/03/2012
44. Source: Bishop John Pritchard, *Going to Church,* 2009, London: SPCK, p.38–40)
45. Nicky Gumbel, *Alpha Questions of Life,* 2007 edition, Eastbourne: Kingsway Communications, p.181.
46. Rick Richardson, 2007, *Re-imagining Evangelism,* Milton Keynes: Scripture Union, p.26–27

Chapter 9

47. Quoted in Bevans and Schroeder (2004), *Constants in Context,* New York: Orbis Books, p.325.
48. http://www.christiantoday.com/article/christians.prefer.friendship.evangelism/31156.htm
49. Rick Richardson, 2006, *Re-imagining Evangelism,* Bletchley, Milton Keynes: Scripture Union, p.23, p69.
50. Source: *EMMAUS the way of truth: Stage 1: Contact,* Church House Publishing, 2003, pp.4,6,13.)
51. Philippians 4:7 (NIV)
52. Source: J. John, *Soul Purpose,* 2008, Milton Keynes: Authentic Media, pp.16–17.)

Chapter 10

53. Surprise Sithole, 2012, *Voice in the Night,* Chosen Books: Michigan USA, p.63
54. Source: Cited in *Alpha Questions of Life,* 2007, Nicky Gumbel, Eastbourne: Kingsway Communications, p.188.
55. *EMMAUS the ways of faith:* Stage 1 Contact. Cottrell, Croft, Finney, Lawson, Warren, London, CHP 2003; p26–27

Appendix 1

56. Stephen Gaukroger, *It Makes Sense,* 2003, Gold Hill, Scripture Union, p.34–34,

57. Philip Yancey, *The Jesus I Never Knew,* 2000, London: Marshall Pickering, p.260

58. Stephen Gaukroger, *It Makes Sense,* p.99–100

Ian Seymour teaches and disciples others in evangelism and undertakes training seminars, workshops and speaking engagements. If you would like to contact Ian email him at rianseymour@gmail.com